MW01492744

Interview Questions for
IBM Mainframe Developers

JCL, VSAM, IMS, DB2, COBOL, PLI, CICS

Robert Wingate

ISBN-13: 978-1539612896

Contents

Disclaimer

The content of this book is based upon the author's understanding of and experience with the IBM mainframe products described herein. Every attempt has been made to provide correct information. However, the author and publisher do not guarantee the accuracy of every detail, nor do they assume responsibility for information included in or omitted from it. All of the information in this book should be used at your own risk.

Copyright

Introduction

Welcome

Congratulations on your purchase of **Interview Questions for IBM Mainframe Application Developers**. This book is meant to help you prepare for your IBM mainframe technical interview. The questions and answers in the book offer you a significant advantage by helping you to test your readiness for that interview, and to help shore up any areas you need help on.

How to Use This Book

I recommend that you use this book as part of a set of resources to assist you in preparing for your technical interview. Regardless of your experience level with the mainframe, the amount of detail in a technical interview can be overwhelming.

I suggest practicing with the IBM mainframe as much as possible. Think up some projects - create a database, some tables, indexes, and views. Create some VSAM files. Add/change/delete data. Write programs in COBOL and/or PLI. Create and use CICS screens. The thing about actually *doing* things is that you'll tend to remember those things more than just reading about it. Isn't this true of most things?

It's my sincere hope that this book will help you in your career with IBM mainframe. I especially hope you ace your application developer technical interview. Good luck!

Robert Wingate
IBM Certified Application Developer – DB2 11 for z/OS

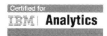

P.S. Thanks for your purchase and if you find this Interview Questions book helpful in preparing for your IBM interview, please leave a positive review at the place you bought it.

I'll really appreciate that!

JCL Questions

1. Which output class will be used when a DD statement is coded with SYSOUT=*.

   It will use the class specified on the MSGCLASS parameter from the JOB statement.

2. If you want to override installation defaults for job processing, which statement would you use?

   The /*JOBPARM statement can be used to override some system defaults. For example, if the installation default for the number of lines to print on a page is 60, you could override it to 50 lines per page by coding:

   ```
   /*JOBPARM  LINECT=50
   ```

3. If you want to submit a job on one system and have it execute on another, what statement could you use?

   You can use the /*ROUTE statement after the job card to send either the job itself to run on another system, or to send the output to another system. Examples:

   ```
   /*ROUTE XEQ SYSTEM2

   /*ROUTE PRINT SYSTEM3
   ```

4. What statement do you use to delimit an instream procedure?

   Use the PEND statement to mark the end of an instream procedure in a JCL.

5. What does the NOTCAT2 error message mean?

   It means you are trying to allocate a dataset, but another dataset with the same name already exists.

6. What does COND=(0,NE) mean?

   Literally it means if zero is not equal to the highest condition code encountered in the job, then do not execute this step. Another way of saying it is the condition code is not equal to zero.

7. What keyword on a SPACE allocation statement returns unused space to the system when the dataset is closed?

   The RLSE keyword frees any allocated but unused space when the dataset is closed.

8. What is the difference between specifying DISP=OLD and DISP=SHR for a Data Set?

   A DISP=OLD means exclusive control of the Data Set; DISP=SHR means access is not exclusive.

9. How is the keyword DUMMY used in JCL?

   It allocates no device for a DD statement. Practically speaking, for an output file, DUMMY specifies that the output is to be discarded. For input, it specifies an empty file.

10. What is the control program used to run a DB2 Program in the EXEC statement of the JCL?

To run a DB2 program under TSO use program IKJEFT01. For example, to run DB2 program PGM0001 in region DB2X from load library PROD.APPL.LOADLIB, use this JCL step:

```
//JS01   EXEC PGM=IKJEFT01,DYNAMNBR=30
//STEPLIB  DD DSN=DB2X.DSNLOAD,DISP=SHR
//         DD DSN=PROD.APPL.LOADLIB,DISP=SHR
 //SYSTSPRT DD SYSOUT=X
 //SYSTSIN  DD *
  DSN SYSTEM(DB2X)
  RUN PROGRAM(PGM0001)  PLAN(PGM0001)
  END
 //SYSPRINT DD SYSOUT=*
```

11. What does the MSGCLASS parameter refer to in JCL?

MSGCLASS determines where the job output is to be printed or held. MSGCLASS values are from A thru Z and 0 to 9. These are system specific, but often MSGCLASS A is used for output directed to the default printer.

12. What does the MSGLEVEL parameter refer to in JCL?

MSGLEVEL indicate which JES statements should be captured. There is a value for statements and a value for messages.

Statements:
0 – Job related statements are printed.
1 – Expanded job statements are printed.
2 – Job input statements are printed.

Messages:

0 – Messages are printed only when the job abends
1 – Messages are printed both times when job abends or successfully completes.
So if you wanted to see all messages, you could code **MSGLEVEL=(1,1)**.

13. How do you reference the latest version of a GDG-based file?

You refer to it as generation zero. For example, the most recent generation of a dataset named XXX.FILE1 would be referenced in JCL as:

```
//DD1 DD DSN=XXX.FILE1(0),DISP=SHR
```

14. What is a way you can find the syntax errors in a JCL without running the job or using a utility?

You can code TYPRUN=SCAN on the JOB statement and submit the job. It will not actually run the jobs steps, but the output will indicate any syntax errors.

15. Explain JOBLIB and STEPLIB in JCL.

JOBLIB specifies the library where the load modules can be found before searching the linklist (i.e., linklist includes the default the system libraries). JOBLIB is coded after the JOB statement and applies to the entire job or JCL.

STEPLIB specifies a load module library but applies only to the step for which it is coded. If both JOBLIB and STEPLIB are coded, the STEPLIB takes precedence over the JOBLIB.

16. How is a temporary dataset coded?

A temporary dataset is coded with the symbols && in front
of a dataset name. Since it is a temporary dataset, it will not
be cataloged. An example is:

```
//DD1   DD   DSN=&&TEMPFILE,DISP=(NEW,PASS),
//           UNIT=SYSDA,SPACE=(TRK,(1,1),RLSE)
//           RECFM=FB,LRECL=80,BLKSIZE=0
```

17. How is the RESTART parameter used in JCL?

RESTART is coded on the JOB statement when there is a
need to restart the job from a particular step. Typically this
will be when a step has abended. The code is:

RESTART=STEPNAME

When you need to restart a job that uses a proc, then the
proc step name must be preceded by the job step name.
For example if the abending job and proc step is JS10 and
PS20 respectively, you would code the following to restart:

RESTART=JS10.PS20

18. Can instream data be used in a PROC?

No, not directly, a proc cannot provide for instream data per
se. However you can code a dummy DD in the proc and
then override it in the JCL. The JCL override can include
instream data. In this way you are passing the JCL's
instream data to the proc.

19. How do you concatenate datasets in JCL?

The first dataset is written as normal, i.e., DDNAME DD DSN=. Any subsequent datasets to be concatenated are added on the following line just like the first the line except you omit the DDNAME. Here's an example:

```
//DDNAME DD DSN=FILE1,DISP=SHR
//       DD DSN=FILE2,DISP=SHR
//       DD DSN=FILE3,DISP=SHR
```

20. How do you reference a new GDG dataset created in an earlier step in the same job.

You refer to it as the +1 generation. A new GDG is created with +1 as the generation and it remains +1 until the end of the job. If you add another generation of the same dataset in the same job, you would use +2 as the generation number, etc.

21. How is the PARM parameter used in JCL?

The PARM parameter passes data from the JCL to an application program. It is coded on the execution EXEC statement as PARM=*parameters to be passed*.

22. What is the TYPRUN parameter used for in JCL.

TYPRUN values are SCAN and HOLD.

TYPRUN=SCAN evaluates the JCL for syntax errors without actually running the job.

TYPRUN=HOLD holds the submitted job and does not run it.

23. How do you communicate the end of instream data in JCL?

To communicate the end of instream data, you code /* in the first 2 columns of the next line after the instream data. For example:

```
//SYSIN     DD *
Data1
Data2
/*
```

24. Explain the use of JCLLIB.

JCLLIB specifies the library where procedures can be found. It is specified after the job statement.

25. How do you designate a comment in JCL?

The comment statement is //* followed by the comments. For example:

//* This is a comment and will not be processed

26. What does a disposition of (NEW, CATLG, DELETE) mean?

This disposition means to allocate a new dataset (NEW). If the job step is successful it will catalog the new dataset (CATLG), and if the job step is not successful it will delete (DELETE) the dataset.

27. When you create a dataset, what keyword do you use in the SPACE parameter if you don't need or want to keep the entire allocation?

Code the RLSE (release) sub-parameter. For example:

```
SPACE=(TRK,(10,5),RLSE)
```

28. Explain the basics of generation data groups.

    A generation data group is a collection of related datasets that use the same base name and can be referenced by generation number. The most recent version of the file is the zero (0) generation. The first previous generation is (-1), the next previous is (-2), etc.

    The absolute file name of each generation is the base GDG file name plus a G00Vxxxx where the xxxx is a sequential number. So the first few generations of a GDG named XXX.FILEABC would be:

    ```
    XXX.FILEABC.G00V0001
    XXX.FILEABC.G00V0002
    XXX.FILEABC.G00V0003
    ```

29. What is primary allocation for a dataset?

    The primary allocation is the space allocated when the dataset is first created.

30. What is the difference between primary and secondary allocations for a dataset?

    Primary allocation is the initial space allocated when the file is created. If additional space is required, the secondary allocation is used up to 16 extents (minus the number of extents used to fill the primary allocation).

31. What does a disposition of (NEW,CATLG,CATLG) mean?

This disposition means to allocate a new dataset (NEW). If the job step is successful it will catalog the new dataset (CATLG), and if the job step is not successful it will also catalog and retain (CATALOG) the dataset. The reasons for specifying CATLG instead of DELETE on an unsuccessful step are debugging and potential restartability.

32. What are the required attributes for an output DD statement?

Unless already allocated earlier, the statement must have a DSN, DISP, UNIT, SPACE and DCB (or the sub-parameters of the DCB: RECFM, LRECL, BLKSIZE).

An example is:

```
//DD1   DD   DSN=XXX.FILE1,
//           DISP=(NEW,CATLG,DELETE),
//           UNIT=SYSDA,
//           SPACE=(TRK,(1,1),RLSE)
//           DCB=(RECFM=FB,
//           LRECL=80,
//           BLKSIZE=0)
```

33. What is DISP= (NEW,PASS,DELETE)?

This means create the file. If the job step is successful, pass the file to subsequent steps. If the job step is not successful then delete the file. Since it is not cataloged, the dataset is deleted at job end.

34. What causes a 'S0C7' abend?

It is a data exception caused by trying to reference or write data of an invalid type into a field that does not accept that type. For example, trying to write character data to a packed numeric field causes a S0C7.

35. What does COND=EVEN mean in JCL?

It means to execute this step even if any of the previous steps abended.

36. What does COND=ONLY mean in JCL?

It means to execute this step only if one of the previous steps abended.

37. What is the purpose of the REGION keyword and what JCL statement is it associated with?

REGION specifies the maximum CPU memory allocated for a particular job or job step. If REGION is on the JOB card, it relates to the entire job. If REGION is on the EXEC statement, it relates to the job step. REGION on the job step overrides the region on the job card.

38. What is the difference between BLKSIZE and LRECL?

LRECL is the logical record length. BLKSIZE refers to how the system physically blocks records for storage on a device. BLKSIZE is required to be multiples of LRECL

39. What is the purpose of the IEFBR14 utility?

IEFBR14 has a variety of uses. Most often it is used to catalog or delete a file. Also, by using (MOD,DELETE,DELETE) **as the disposition, IEFBR14 first creates the catalog entry for the file if it does not already exist. Why do it this way? Because it is flexible, allowing for the possibility that the files to be deleted do not actually exist every time the job runs. If the files do exist, they get deleted. If they do not exist, you prevent a runtime error (trying to delete a non-existent file) by specifying MOD as the first sub-parameter of the disposition.**

40. What is the main difference on a DD statement between creating a new sequential flat file and a partitioned dataset?

The SPACE=(n,m) for a sequential file, SPACE=(n,m,p) for a PDS where n is the primary space allocation, m is the secondary space allocation, and p specifies the number of directory blocks to allocate.

41. What does the following statement mean?

```
        SYSIN  DD   *
```

Instream data follows, and is terminated when a line containing /* in columns 1 and 2 is encountered.

42. What does the OUTLIM sub-parameter do?

It specifies the maximum number of records to be written to a sysout DD. This is mostly used to prevent wasted space or print when an abend occurs and there is a huge dump.

Here is an example that limits the output of the
SYSUDUMP DD to 2000 lines:

```
//SYSUDUMP  DD SYSOUT=A,OUTLIM=2000
```

43. What does the SET statement do?

    It assigns values to symbolic parameters. In the following
    example, &DNS1 is replaced by XXX. PROD:

```
//AB12   SET DSN1="XXX.PROD"
//RPT        DD DSN=&DSN1.REPORT,DISP=SHR
```

44. What IDCAMS keyword do you specify to copy a file?

    REPRO is used to copy a file. A coding example is:

```
//***********************************************
//* IDCAMS TO COPY A DATA SET
//***********************************************
//*
//STEP1     EXEC PGM=IDCAMS
//SYSPRINT  DD SYSOUT=*
//SYSUDUMP  DD SYSOUT=*
//FILEIN    DD DSN=DSNAME.TEST.FILE,DISP=SHR
//FILEOUT   DD DSN=DSNAME.TEST.FILE2,
//             DISP=(NEW,CATLG,DELETE),
//             UNIT=SYSDA,
//             SPACE=(TRK,(5,5),RLSE),
//             RECFM=FB,LRECL=4096,BLKSIZE=4096
//SYSIN     DD *
 REPRO INFILE (FILEIN) OUTFILE (FILEOUT)
/*
//
```

45. What IDCAMS keywords would you use to copy a file, to omit the first 1000 records, and to stop after the next 500 records?

The keywords are SKIP and COUNT. Here are the control statements, and note the continuation character - :

```
//SYSIN      DD *
      REPRO   INFILE(FILEIN)    -
              OUTFILE(FILEOUT) -
              SKIP  (1000)      -
              COUNT (500)
//SYSPRINT  DD SYSOUT=*
//SYSUDUMP  DD SYSOUT=*
//
```

Notice the continuation character dash – is used to continue the command across several lines.

46. Which IBM JCL utility is used to duplicate a partitioned dataset?

IEBCOPY is used to copy a partitioned dataset. Here is a code example that copies PDS DSNAME.PDS.FILE to DSNAME.PDS.FILE.BACKUP:

```
//*
//STEP1      EXEC PGM=IEBCOPY
//SYSIN      DD *
  COPY INDD=SYSUT1,OUTDD=SYSUT2
/*
//SYSUT1    DD DSN=DSNAME.PDS.FILE,DISP=SHR
//SYSUT2    DD DSN=DSNAME.PDS.FILE.BACKUP,
//             DISP=(NEW,CATLG,DELETE),
//             UNIT=TAPE,RECFM=FB,LRECL=80,
//             DSORG=PO,BLKSIZE=27920
//SYSUT3    DD UNIT=SYSDA,
//             SPACE=(TRK,(100,100),RLSE)
//SYSUT4    DD UNIT=SYSDA,
//             SPACE=(TRK,(100,100),RLSE)
//SYSPRINT  DD SYSOUT=*
//SYSUDUMP  DD SYSOUT=*
```

47. How can you check if a file is empty using JCL?

**When the file is used as input in IDCAMS, the job
completes with a warning (return code 04) if the file is
empty. You can use a dummied output file and not have to
allocate it.**

Here is a code example:

```
//STEP1     EXEC PGM=IDCAMS
//SYSUDUMP  DD SYSOUT=*
//SYSPRINT  DD SYSOUT=*
//FILEIN    DD DSN=DSNAME.TEST.FILE1,
//             DISP=SHR
//FILEOUT   DD DUMMY,RECFM=FB,
//             LRECL=80,BLKSIZE=8000
//SYSIN     DD *
      REPRO    INFILE(FILEIN) -
               OUTFILE(FILEOUT) -
               COUNT(1)
/*
```

48. How do you catalog an uncataloged dataset with a JCL?

**By using the UNIT and VOL serial parameter in the dataset
DD statement, and specifying disposition** (OLD,CATLG,DELETE).
For example:

```
//*
//****************************************************************
//* DEFINE GDG BASE AND A MODEL DATA SET
//****************************************************************
//STEP10    EXEC PGM=IEFBR14
//SYSPRINT  DD SYSOUT=*
//SYSOUT    DD SYSOUT=*
//DD1       DD DSN=XXXXXX.TEST.FILE,
//             DISP=(OLD,CATLG,DELETE),
//             UNIT=3390,VOL=SER=DEVMA5
```

49. What are some capabilities of the IDCAMS utility in JCL?

IDCAMS has a number of functions. Some of these are:

- **Copy VSAM and NON VSAM Datasets (REPRO)**
- **Create GDG**
- **Delete GDG**
- **Rename a dataset**
- **Create a VSAM dataset (Define Cluster)**
- **To run a LISTCAT**

VSAM Questions

1. What are the three types of VSAM datasets?

    Entry-sequenced datasets (ESDS), key-sequenced datasets (KSDS) and relative record dataset (RRDS).

2. How are records stored in an ESDS (entry sequenced) dataset?

    They are stored in the order in which they are inserted into the file.

3. What VSAM feature enables you to access the records in a KSDS dataset based on a key that is different than the file's primary key?

    VSAM allows creation of an alternate index which enables you to access the records in a KSDS dataset based on that alternate index rather than the primary key.

4. What is a cluster?

    A cluster is another name for a VSAM file. A KSDS cluster consists of a data component and an index component.

5. What is the general purpose utility program that provides services for VSAM files?

   Access Method Services is the utility program that provides services for VSAM files. Often it is referred to as IDCAMS which is the executable program in batch.

6. What is a control interval?

   A control interval is the unit of data that VSAM uses and is similar to blocking for non-VSAM files. It consists of three parts: logical records, control information and free space.

7. What is a spanned record?

   A spanned record is a record that is longer than the control interval, hence it spans more than one control interval.

8. What are the two parts of a KSDS index?

   A KSDS index consists of a sequence set and an index set. For random access, the sequence set must be searched to determine which control interval a record resides in. The index set includes entries that point to the sequence set records.

9. What are the two ways you can reserve space in a KSDS when it is created?

   You can leave unused space within each control interval, and you can leave entire control intervals empty.

10. What is a base cluster?

   A base cluster refers to the data set that comprises an alternate index.

11. Which AMS function lists information about datasets?

   The LISTCAT function lists information about datasets. An example is:

```
//STEP1     EXEC PGM=IDCAMS
//SYSPRINT  DD SYSOUT=X
//SYSIN     DD *
 LISTCAT GDG ENT('DSNAME.GDGFILE.TEST1') ALL
```

12. If you are mostly going to use a KSDS file for sequential access, should you define a larger or smaller control interval when creating the file?

   For sequential access a larger control interval is desirable for performance because you maximize the data brought in with each I/O.

13. What is the basic AMS command to create a VSAM file?

   DEFINE CLUSTER is the basic command to create a VSAM file.

14. To use the REWRITE command in COBOL, the VSAM file must be opened in what mode?

   To use the REWRITE command in COBOL, the VSAM file must be opened for I/O.

15. Which AMS command copies data from one file to another?

The REPRO command copies data from one file to another. For example:

```
//STEP1     EXEC PGM=IDCAMS
//SYSPRINT  DD SYSOUT=*
//SYSUDUMP  DD SYSOUT=*
//FILEIN    DD DSN=DSNAME.TEST.FILE,DISP=SHR
//FILEOUT   DD DSN=DSNAME.TEST.FILE2,
//             DISP=(NEW,CATLG,DELETE),
//             UNIT=SYSDA,
//             SPACE=(TRK,(5,5),RLSE),
//             RECFM=FB,LRECL=4096,BLKSIZE=4096
//SYSIN     DD *
 REPRO INFILE (FILEIN) OUTFILE (FILEOUT)
/*
//
```

16. Which AMS command is used to create an alternate index?

The DEFINE ALTERNATEINDEX command is used to create an alternate index. In this example a secondary index EMPLOYEE.SSNINDX is created on the EMPLOYEE base cluster and let's assume the alternate key is located at a displacement of 31 bytes and is 9 characters long. The secondary key is non unique. The secondary index file will be opened every time the base cluster EMPLOYEE.KSDS is opened.

```
//STEP1     EXEC  PGM=IDCAMS
//SYSPRINT DD     SYSOUT=A
//SYSIN    DD     *
         DEFINE ALTERNATEINDEX -
              (NAME(EMPLOYEE.SSNINDX) -
              RELATE(EMPLOYEE.KSDS) -
              KEYS(9 10) -
              RECORDSIZE(40 50) -
              VOLUMES(VSER01) -
              CYLINDERS(9 31) -
              NONUNIQUEKEY -
              UPGRADE) -
              CATALOG(USERCAT)
```

17. When running IDCAMS, what is the main difference between return code 08 and return code 12?

Return code 08 means a major problem was encountered but the command may have been completed. Return code 12 means a major problem was encountered and the command could not be completed.

18. What is a control interval split?

If there isn't enough space in the control interval VSAM performs a control interval split by moving some records to the free control intervals. If there isn't a free control interval VSAM performs a control area split by allocating a new control area and moving half of the control intervals to it.

19. When creating a VSAM file, how does the OWNER parameter influence how the file is processed?

The OWNER parameter is for documentation only and does not affect how the file is created or processed.

20. If you don't specify a CATALOG parameter when creating a file, what determines the catalog that will own the file?

If you don't specify a CATALOG parameter when creating a file, the high level qualifier of the dataset name is used to identify the catalog that owns the file.

21. What is a control area?

A control area is a group of control intervals.

22. What does a file status error code 22 mean?

   It means duplicate key, i.e., you tried to write a record with a key that is already present in the file.

23. What is the catalog?

   A catalog includes the names of all datasets, both VSAM and non-VSAM. It is used to access these datasets.

24. What is a path?

   A path is a file that allows you to access a file by alternate index - the path provides an association between the alternate index and the base cluster.

25. What is the upgrade set?

   An upgrade set is the list of all alternate indexes that VSAM must maintain for a specific base cluster.

26. You can create a model KSDS to use it's values for all new KSDS data sets. Assume you name such a model file as PROD.KSDS.MODEL, how do you specify use of that model file when creating a new KSDS file?

   You specify MODEL(PROD.KSDS.MODEL) in the DEFINE CLUSTER action for the new file. You can then include the parameter names and values for any parameters you want to override.

27. When you define an alternate index, what is the function of the RELATE parameter?

The RELATE parameter associates your alternate index with the base cluster that you are creating the alternate index for.

28. When you define a path using DEFINE PATH, what does the PATHENTRY parameter do?

The PATHENTRY parameter includes the name of the alternate index that you are cresting the path for.

29. After you've defined an alternate index and path, what AMS command must you issue to actually populate the alternate index?

Issue the BLXINDEX command to populate an alternate index.

30. After you've created a VSAM file, if you need to add additional DASD volumes that can be used with that file, what command would you?

Use an ALTER command and specify the keyword ADDVOLUMES(XXX001 YYY002) where XXX001 and YYY002 are DASD volume names.

31. If you want to set a VSAM file to read only status, what command would you use?

Use the **ALTER** command with the **INHIBIT** keyword.
For example:

```
//STEP1 EXEC PGM=IDCAMS
//SYSPRINT DD SYSOUT=*
//SYSIN DD *
ALTER -
PROD.EMPL.DATA -
INHIBIT
ALTER -
PROD.EMPL.INDEX -
INHIBIT
/*
```

To return the file to read/update, use **ALTER** with the
UNINHIBIT keyword.

32. If you are mostly going to use a KSDS file for random access,
should you define a larger or smaller control interval?

**For random access a smaller control interval is desirable
for performance because you minimize the unneeded
data records brought back in I/O.**

33. If you see FREESPACE (20 10), what does this mean?

**It means that in each control interval 20 percent of the
space is reserved for new records, and 10 percent of the
control intervals in the control area are reserved for new
data.**

34. What are some ways you can improve the performance of a KSDS file?

- **Ensure that the control interval is optimally sized (smaller for random access and larger for sequential access).**

- **Allocate additional index buffers to reduce data I/Os by keeping needed records in virtual storage.**

- **Ensure sufficient free space in control intervals to avoid control interval splits.**

35. Do primary key values in a KSDS have to be unique?

Yes the primary key has to be unique. However, alternate index values need not be unique. For example if an EMPLOYEE file uses employee number as the primary key, then the employee number must be unique. However the EMPLOYEE file could be alternately indexed on department. In this case, the department need not be unique.

36. What does a file status error code 23 mean?

It means you tried to access a record that does not exist.

37. In the COBOL SELECT statement what organization should be specified for a KSDS file?

In a COBOL SELECT statement, the organization for a KSDS file is INDEXED.

38. Name some of the IDCAMS commands and what they do.

The IDCAMS commands and what they do are as follows:

- **REPRO copies the contents of one file to another.**
- **DEFINE is used for ALTERNATEINDEX, CLUSTER or PATH commands.**
- **DELETE removes a catalog entry.**
- **PRINT prints the contents of a dataset.**
- **BLDINDEX builds an alternate index.**
- **ALTER modifies information for a catalog, alternate index, cluster or path.**
- **LISTCAT lists information about the dataset.**

39. In the COBOL SELECT statement for a KSDS what are the three possibilities for ACCESS?

In the COBOL SELECT statement for a KSDS, ACCESS can be SEQUENTIAL, RANDOM or DYNAMIC.

40. What are the three levels of definition for the VSAM DEFINE command?

The three levels of definition for the VSAM DEFINE command are CLUSTER, DATA and INDEX.

41. With IDCAMS you can perform multiple functions in one job step and each has its own return code. If the return codes for each function are different, what condition code is returned to the operating system?

The highest condition code generated is returned as the condition code of the IDCAMS step.

42. What is the COBOL RECORD KEY clause used for?

The RECORD KEY clause specifies the files primary key as used in the program.

43. How do you load a VSAM data set with records?

Use IDCAMS with the REPRO command.

44. What does the KEYRANGES parameter in a Define Cluster command do and why would you use it?

It divides a large file into several volumes according to the key ranges specified. For example you could specify KEYRANGES ((0001 3999) (4000 5999)). This makes concurrent access possible, thereby improving performance.

45. By default how many buffers are allotted to a VSAM KSDS?

For a KSDS, by default VSAM allocates two data buffers and one index buffer.

46. If you are adding records to a VSAM KSDS and receive return code 28, what does that mean?

   Return code 28 means the out of space condition was raised.

47. Is there a performance penalty for using an alternate index compared to using the primary key?

   Yes because if you access a record through an ALTERNATE INDEX, the alternate key must first be located and then it points to the primary key entry which is finally used to locate the actual record.

48. What must be done to use an alternate index in a CICS program?

   You must create FCT entries for the base cluster and the path.

49. What file status code will you receive if an operation succeeded?

   If an operation succeeded without any problem you will receive a 00 file status code.

50. What is a Relative Byte Address?

   The Relative Byte Address (RBA) indicates in bytes how far a record is displaced from the beginning of the file.

IMS Questions

1. What is the name of the interface program you call from a PL/1 program to perform IMS operations?

   PLITDLI is the normal interface program for a PL/1 program to access IMS.   There is also a PLIHSSR interface that is only used with the IBM High Speed Sequential Retrieval utility.

2. Here are some IMS return codes and . Explain briefly what each of them means: blank, GE, GB, II

   > **Blank – successful operation**
   > **GE – segment not found**
   > **GB – end of database**
   > **II – duplicate key, insert failed**

3. What is an SSA?

   Segment Search Argument – it is used to select segments by name and to specify search criteria for specific segments.

4. Briefly explain these entities: DBD, PSB, PCB?

   A Database Description (DBD) specifies characteristics of a database. The name, parent, and length of each segment type in the database.

   A Program Specification Block (PSB) is the program view of one or more IMS databases. The PSB includes one or more program communication blocks (PCB) for each IMS database that the program needs access to.

A Program Communication Block (PCB) specifies the database to be accessed, the processing options such as read-only or various updating options, and the database segments that can be accessed.

5. What is the use of CMPAT parameter in PSB ?

It is required if you are going to run your program in Batch Mode Processing (BMP), that is - in the online region. If you always run the program in DL/I mode, you do not need the CMPAT. If you are going to run BMP, you need the CMPAT=YES specified in the PSB.

6. What is the difference between IMS-DC and IMS-DB?

IMS DB (database) manages the IMS databases. It is used for physical storage of data, and for data retrieval.

IMS DC (data communications) is the online transaction processing system.

7. What is the difference between twin segments and sibling segments?

Twin segments are segments of the same type under the same root. Sibling segments are segments of different types under the same root.

8. Explain what the OLDS refers to?

OLDS is the online log data set which records the information necessary to restart the system if a system failure occurs. There are usually more than one **OLDS** so that when one is full **IMS** switches to another.

9. In IMS, what is the difference between a key field and a search field?

A key field is used to make the record unique and to order the database. A search field is a field that is needed to search the database on but does not have to be unique and does not order the database. For example, an **EMPLOYEE** database might be keyed on unique **EMP-NUMBR**. A search field might be needed on **PHONE-NUMBER** or **ZIP-CODE**. Even though the database is not ordered by these fields, they can be made search fields to query the database.

10. What does PROCOPT mean in a PCB?

The **PROCOPT** parameter specifies *processing options* that are allowed for this **PCB** when operating on a segment.

The different **PROCOPT**s and their meaning are:

    G - Get segment from **DB**
    I - Insert segment into **DB**
    R - Replace segment
    D - Delete segment
    A - All the above operations

11. Name a few advantages of using a secondary index.

Advantages of using a secondary index include:

- **Fast access by a key other than the primary key. Especially important in an online environment.**

- **It is possible to do an index-only scan if the information needed is all in the index. This improves performance.**

- **Indexing is not limited to root segments. You can index child segments so that access by the secondary index avoid traversing the entire DB hierarchy.**

12. What is the main difference between HDAM and HIDAM storage where it concerns the primary key field?

HIDAM stores the records in primary key order. HDAM typically uses a randomizer to determine where to store records so they are not stored in order of primary key.

13. Which is more efficient, HDAM or HIDAM?

It depends on the access requirements. HDAM is the most efficient unless there is a requirement to do heavy sequential processing of the database. In the latter case, HIDAM is usually more efficient because the records are organized in key sequence.

14. What are the four parameters of a DLI retrieval call?

- **Function**
- **PCB**
- **SSAs**
- **IO Area**

15. What are Qualified SSA and Unqualified SSA?

   A qualified SSA specifies the segment type and the specific instance (key) of the segment to be returned. An unqualified SSA simply supplies the name of the segment type that you want to operate upon. You could use the latter if you don't care which specific segment you retrieve.

16. Which PSB parameter in a PSBGEN specifies the language in which the application program is written?

   The LANG parameter specifies the language in which the application program is written. Examples:

   ```
   LANG=COBOL
   LANG=PLI
   LANG=ASSEM
   ```

17. What does SENSEG stand for and how is it used in a PCB?

   SENSEG is known as Segment Level Sensitivity. It defines the program's access to parts of the database and it is identified at the segment level. For example, PROCOPT=G on a SENSEG means the segment is read-only by this PCB.

18. What are the processing modes available in IMS DB?

Batch DL/I
MPP Mode - (Message Processing Program)
BMP Mode - (Batch Message Processing)

19. What storage mechanism/format is used for IMS index databases?

IMS index databases must use VSAM KSDS.

20. What are the DL/I commands to add, change and remove a segment?

The following are the DL/I commands for adding, changing and removing a segment:

- **ISRT**
- **REPL**
- **DLET**

21. What return code will you receive from IMS if the DL/I call was successful?

IMS returns blanks/spaces in the PCB STATUS-CODE field when the call was successful.

22. If you want to retrieve the last occurrence of a child segment under its parent, what command code could you use?

   Use the L command code to retrieve the last child segment under its parent. Incidentally, IMS ignores the L command code at the root level.

23. When would you use a GU call?

   GU is used to retrieve a segment occurrence based on SSA supplied arguments.

24. When would you use a GHU call?

   GHU (Get Hold Unique) retrieves and locks the record that you intend to update or delete.

25. What order is the predefined pattern for traversing a database using sequential processing?

   The pattern for sequential traversal of an IMS database is top to bottom, left to right, front to back.

26. What is the difference between running an IMS program as DLI and BMP ?

   DLI runs within its own address space. BMP runs under the IMS online control region. The practical difference concerns programs that update the database. If performing updates, DLI requires exclusive use of the database. Running BMP does not require exclusive use because it runs under control of the online region.

27. When would you use a GNP call?

The GNP call is used for Get Next within Parent. This function is used to retrieve segment occurrences in sequence subordinate to an established parent segment.

28. What are the IMS commands used to process GSAM files?

The IMS commands to process a GSAM file are:

- **OPEN – explicitly opens the GSAM file.**

- **CLSE – explicitly closes the GSAM file.**

- **GN – retrieves the next sequential record from the file into the I/O area.**

- **ISRT – inserts a record at the end of the file.**

29. Which IMS call is used to restart an abended program?

The XRST IMS call is made to restart an abended IMS program. Assuming the program has taken checkpoints during the abended program execution, the XRST call is used to restart from the last checkpoint taken instead of starting the processing all over.

30. What is the main advantage of using GSAM data sets?

The Generalized Sequential Access Method enables program restartability for regular sequential z/OS files (sometimes referred to as flat files).

31. What does the CBLTDLI IMS call do?

CBLTDLI stands for COBOL to DL/I. It is an interface module that is link edited with the program's object module so it can request DL/I services.

32. How do you establish parentage on a segment occurrence?

By issuing a successful GU or GN (or GHU or GHN) call that retrieves the segment on which the parentage is to be established. IMS normally sets parentage at the lowest level segment retrieved in a call. If you want to establish parentage at a level other than the normal level, use the P command code.

33. What is a checkpoint?

A checkpoint is a stage where the modifications done to a database by an application program are considered complete and are committed to the database with the CHKP IMS call.

34. Enumerate and explain the MFS control blocks.

MFS control blocks are the MOD, MID, DIF and DOF.

MOD – the message output descriptor defines the layout of messages the application program sends to MFS.

MID - the message input descriptor defines the layout of messages the application program receives from MFS.

DOF – the device output format is how **MFS** formats messages for the device the program is sending data to (such as a terminal).

DIF – the device input format defines the messages the device (such as a terminal) sends to **MFS**.

35. What is the difference between the ROLL call and the ROLB call?

    ROLB means that any changes are backed out to the last checkpoint, and then control is returned to the calling program which can continue processing. ROLL means that any changes are backed out to the last checkpoint, and then the program is terminated with abend code U0778.

36. Which is the first statement in the PROCEDURE DIVISION of a COBOL-IMS program?

    The ENTRY statement is the first statement after the procedure division of a COBOL-IMS program.

37. What does the P command code accomplish?

    The P command code sets parentage at a level other than the normal level (the normal level being the lowest segment level in the most recent retrieval call).

    For example if you had a three level hierarchy with segment types SEG01, SEG02, SEG03 representing the three levels, you could do a GU call to a SEG03 level. If your SSA for the SEG01 level (the root segment) contains a P command code, then parentage IS SET AT THE ROOT LEVEL.

38. What termination statement in COBOL causes control of an IMS program to be returned to the IMS control program?

The GOBACK statement in COBOL causes control to be returned to the IMS control program. In PLI you would use RETURN.

39. How do you update the primary key of an IMS segment?

You cannot update the primary key of a segment. If the key on a record must be changed, you can DLET the existing segment and then ISRT a new segment with the new key.

40. Do you need to use a qualified SSA with REPL/DLET calls?

No, you don't need to include an SSA with REPL/DLET calls. This is because the target segment has already been retrieved and held by a get hold call (that is the only way you can update or delete a segment).

41. If you have a program that needs to retrieve data using a new secondary index, what you need to change in the PSB?

The PSBGEN for the program must specify the proper processing sequence for the data base on the PROCSEQ parameter of the PCB macro. To use a secondary index, PROCSEQ must be set to the DBD name of the secondary index.

42. What is a root segment?

A segment that lies at the top of the hierarchy is called the root segment. It is the only segment through which all dependent segments are accessed.

43. What are twin segments?

Two or more segment occurrences of a particular segment type under a single parent segment occurrence are called twin segments.

44. What are command codes?

Command codes are used along with SSAs to perform additional operations.

Common command codes used are:

> **'P' - used to set parentage on a particular segment.**
> **'D' - used for path calls, to retrieve the entire hierarchical path.**

45. What IBM tool can be used to test IMS programs from a TSO terminal?

You can use Batch Terminal Simulator (BTS) to test IMS programs from a TSO terminal.

46. What are some advantages to using Batch Terminal Simulator?

Some advantages of BTS are:

- **No program code changes are required to test IMS programs.**
- **You can access the DL/I databases from a TSO session.**
- **BTS is robust – you can test any aspect of the IMS program, including logic, communications and interfaces.**

47. What are some components/features and advantages of an IMS SYSPLEX environment?

   Components are data sharing and distribution of the workload across the SYSPLEX. The advantages are high availability, balancing of workloads and optimizing capacity.

DB2 Questions

1. What are some factors that cause a cursor to be ambiguous?

   An ambiguous cursor is one in which **DB2** cannot tell if the cursor is used for updates, or for read operations only. Factors making a cursor ambiguous include the following:

   - It is defined without a **FOR FETCH ONLY, FOR UPDATE** or **FOR READ ONLY** clause.

   - It is not defined on a read-only result table.

   - It is not the target of a **WHERE CURRENT** clause on an **SQL UPDATE** or **DELETE** statement.

   - It is in a plan or package that contains the **SQL** statements **PREPARE** or **EXECUTE IMMEDIATE**.

2. Name and describe the major types of constraints related to tables.

   - A **UNIQUE** constraint requires that the value in a particular field in a table be unique for each record.

   - A **REFERENTIAL** constraint enforces relationships between tables. For example you can define a referential constraint between an **EMPLOYEES** table and a **DEPARTMENTS** table, such that a **DEPT** field in the **EMPLOYEES** table can only contain a value that matches a key value in the **DEPARTMENT** table.

- A **CHECK** constraint establishes some condition on a field, such as **>= 10.**

- **A NOT NULL** constraint establishes that each record must have a non-null value for this field.

3. Name several benefits of using indexes.

   - **Indexes can enforce uniqueness.**
   - **Indexes provide efficiency in looking up records in large tables.**
   - **Indexes can facilitate ORDER BY operations because they represent a logical ordering of the records.**
   - **Indexes support clustered storage which forces physical ordering of records.**

4. Name some ways you can check for processing errors in your DB2 application program?

   - **Typically you would check for specific values in the SQLCODE to determine if there are any errors.**

   - **Use the WHENEVER statement with NOTFOUND, SQLERROR and SQLWARNING values to flag and handle unexpected conditions.**

   - **The DSNTIAR utility enables you to get a formatted output of the SQLCA and a text message based on the SQLCODE field.**

5. Name and explain the various types of joins.

- An **INNER** join returns only those records which meet the join condition, e.g. **TABLE1 INNER JOIN TABLE2 on TABLE1_FIELD = TABLE2_FIELD.**

- A **FULL OUTER** join includes all records in both tables that meet the select criteria.

- A **LEFT OUTER** join includes all records in the "left" table that meet the search criteria, plus matching records in the "right" table that meet the search criteria.

- A **RIGHT OUTER** join includes all records in the "right" table that meet the search criteria, plus matching records in the "left" table that meet the search criteria.

6. Explain a case in which you would NOT want to use static SQL?

You would not want to use static **SQL** when you don't know the structure of your **SQL** beforehand. To run static **SQL** you must know the structure of the **SQL** statements you are going to embed in your program.

7. Which conditions can be trapped using the WHENEVER embedded SQL clause, and what keywords describe the conditions?

The conditions are NOT FOUND, SQLWARNING and SQLERROR.

- **NOT FOUND refers to a condition resulting in SQLCODE +100.**

- **SQLERROR occurs when any condition results in a negative SQLCODE.**

- **SQLWARNING occurs when any condition results in a positive SQLCODE other than +100.**

8. Explain the use of a DCLGEN. What is it and what is it used for?

DCLGEN is an IBM utility that generates SQL data structures (table definition and host variables) for a table or view, stores it in a PDS and then that member can be included in a PL/1 or COBOL program. INCLUDE can then be used to embed the generated structure into the program. For example, assuming the structure is in member MEMBER1 of the PDS, the statement EXEC SQL INCLUDE MEMBER1 will include the SQL structures in the program.

9. Briefly explain the pre-compile, bind package and bind plan process.

The DB2 related steps for program preparation are:

- **Precompile SQL which produces a DBRM**
- **Bind package using the DBRM**
- **Bind plan specifying the package(s)**

10. If you want a cursor to account for records added by another application after your cursor is opened, what clauses are needed?

If you declare your cursor as SENSITIVE DYNAMIC, then all committed inserts, updates, and deletes made by other application processes are visible to your application program.

11. You wish to use static SQL in a Java application. Which programming interface would accomplish this?

Java applications use the SQLJ interface for static SQL. The JDBC interface is used for dynamic SQL.

12. If you want to run a DB2 package on a server other than a DB2-for-z/OS server, which value should you use for the pre-compile SQL option?

SQL(ALL) means any SQL statement that meets the rules for DRDA will be accepted, so this is the one you should use. The alternative is SQL(DB2) means any statement that does not follow the rules of DB2 for z/OS will not be accepted. So you would not want to use this option if your SQL is going to execute on a non-DB2 for z/OS server.

13. When binding a package, what are the performance-guided recommended values for ISOLATION and CURRENTDATA for most applications?

The recommended values for these options with most applications are:

`ISOLATION(CS)` and `CURRENTDATA(NO)`

These settings enable DB2 to acquire the least locks and to release the locks more quickly than all settings except ISOLATION(UR) - Uncomitted Read. Since this last setting allows the application to read uncommitted (dirty) data, it is not usually preferred. The RS and RR isolation levels acquire more locks and hold them longer, so they are not optimal for performance.

The CURRENTDATA(YES) setting means that (for local tables) the data upon which the cursor is positioned cannot change while the cursor is positioned on it, hence this setting causes more locks than the CURRENTDATA(NO) setting. So the CURRENTDATA(NO) setting is usually preferred.

14. What is the correct syntax to create a user-defined global variable?

Use the CREATE VARIABLE statement to create a user-defined global variable. For example, you could create TEST_VAR as follows:

```
CREATE VARIABLE
TEST_VAR VARCHAR(10)
DEFAULT 'TEST VALUE';
```

15. Which EXPLAIN table includes information about the access path that will be used to return data?

The PLAN_TABLE includes information about access paths that is derived from the explain statements.

16. If you find out that your application query is doing a full table space scan, what change should you make to improve the scan efficiency?

You should create one or more indexes on the search columns so that an index scan would occur instead of the tablespace scan.

17. What command would be used to initiate a DB2 accounting trace?

To initiate a DB2 accounting trace, you would issue this abbreviated command:

   STA TRA (ACCTG)

You could also issue START TRACE (ACCTG) which has the same meaning.

18. Assume you want to create an index-only access path where you can retrieve the index key plus one or two non-indexed columns with the same query. The additional columns are not to be used to enforce uniqueness. How can you accomplish this?

Include the non-indexed columns with INCLUDE (<column>) in the unique index definition. This will append the included columns to the index but it will not use them to enforce uniqueness. This is sometimes done when

a field is almost always needed in most queries against the table. In cases where all the data elements requested are stored in the index, then the query can be satisfied by index-only access path, thus improving performance.

19. Name some ways of discouraging the DB2 Optimizer from choosing a SORT access path?

- **Add an index that includes the columns that would otherwise need to be sorted. If an index is available that includes the columns in the same ORDER BY sequence, it will likely be selected to order the results instead of doing a SORT.**

- **The OPTIMIZE FOR 1 ROW specifically requests DB2 to choose an access path that avoids a sort.**

- **A reverse scan is possible on an ascending index that orders the data opposite of what is requested in the ORDER BY. So if a query requests the data to be ordered A, B, C descending and there is an A, B, C ascending ordered index, a sort can be avoided by specifying: ORDER BY A, B, C DESC.**

20. To end a transaction without making the changes permanent, which DB2 statement should be issued?

Issuing a ROLLBACK statement will end a transaction without making the changes permanent.

21. If you want to maximize data concurrency without seeing uncommitted data, which isolation level should you use?

You should use CS (Cursor Stability). CURSOR STABILITY only locks the row where the cursor is placed, thus maximizing concurrency compared to RR (Repeatable Read) or RS Read Stability). UR (UNCOMMITTED READ) permits reading of uncommitted data and the question specifically disallows that.

22. Assume you have a long running process and you want to commit results after processing every 500 records, but still want the ability to undo any work that has taken place after the commit point. What mechanism could you use to do this?

Issuing a SAVEPOINT enables you to execute several SQL statements as a single executable block. You can then undo changes back out to that savepoint by issuing a ROLLBACK TO SAVEPOINT statement.

23. Name some ways that a unit of work is ended.

A commit, a rollback, or the end of an application process can end a unit of work.

24. In an IMS program that makes updates to DB2 tables, what call is required to make data changes permanent?

The checkpoint call CHKP is required to make DB2 data changes permanent. If you issue a DB2 COMMIT statement it will have no affect in an IMS program.

25. Which isolation levels enable you to use the SKIP LOCKED DATA clause on a SELECT statement?

To use SKIP LOCKED DATA the application must use either cursor stability (CS) or read stability (RS) isolation level. The SKIP LOCKED DATA clause is ignored if the isolation level is uncommitted read (UR) or repeatable read (RR).

26. Which value of the RELEASE bind option ensures that resources are released only after the thread terminates?

Specifying RELEASE(DEALLOCATE) means resources will be released when the thread terminates.

FYI, specifying RELEASE(COMMIT) means resources will be released after each commit point.

27. Assume you are doing a multi-row INSERT and have specified NOT ATOMIC CONTINUE ON SQLEXCEPTION. On the INSERT of one of the rows, a -803 is returned. What will the result be for this transaction?

When the NOT ATOMIC CONTINUE ON SQLEXCEPTION clause is specified in the INSERT statement, any row causing a SQL exception will not be inserted but all the other rows are still inserted.

28. Order the isolation levels, from greatest to least impact on performance.

RR, RS, CS, UR.

Repeatable Read has the greatest impact on performance because it incurs the most overhead and locks the most rows. It ensures that a query issued multiple times within the same unit of work will produce the exact same results. It does this by locking all rows that could affect the result, and does not permit any adds/changes/deletes to the table that could affect the result.

READ STABILITY locks for the duration of the transaction those rows that are returned by a query, but it allows additional rows to be added to the table.

CURSOR STABILITY only locks the row that the cursor is placed on (and any rows it has updated during the unit of work).

UNCOMMITTED READ permits reading of uncommitted changes which may never be applied to the database and does not lock any rows at all unless the row(s) is updated during the unit of work.

29. In an IMS program, to roll back changes to the last commit point and return control to the calling program, which IMS call is appropriate?

The correct answer is ROLB. ROLB means that any changes are backed out to the last checkpoint, and then control is returned to the calling program which can continue processing. ROLL means that any changes are backed out to the last checkpoint, and then the program is terminated with abend code U0778.

30. What are some ways that you can test a DB2 SQL statement?

- **You can run the statement from the DB2 command line processor.**

- **You can run the statement from the SPUFI utility.**

- **You can run the statement from IBM Data Studio.**

31. Which bind option would you use to enable parallel processing for static SQL?

When using static SQL you can enable parallel processing by including the DEGREE(ANY) bind option/value.

Note: Issuing SQL statement SET CURRENT DEGREE='ANY' would only affect dynamic SQL statements, not static SQL.

32. Which SQL error code indicates a DB2 package is not found within the DB2 plan?

The -805 SQLCODE indicates that the specified package was not found in the DB2 plan. Typically this requires a BIND PACKAGE action to resolve.

33. Which function reads data from a delimiter-separated file in the Hadoop Distributed File System?

The HDFS_READ function reads data from a delimiter-separated file in the Hadoop Distributed File System.

34. Which function can be used to retrieve/modify data from a JSON document?

Use the JSON_VAL function to retrieve data that is inside a JSON document. The syntax for JSON_VAL is:

```
JSON_VAL(json-value,search-string,result-type)
```

35. Which XQuery expression returns true or false depending on whether at least one record satisfies the query?

XMLEXISTS() returns the values True or False depending on whether at least one row satisfies the query.

36. What are two functions used to access data in a Hadoop system?

The JAQL_SUBMIT function allows you to invoke an InfoSphere BigInsights ad hoc Jaql query from a DB2 application. This function creates a CSV file from JSON data as input for the HDFS_READ function.

The HDFS_READ function reads data from the CSV file.

37. Explain the various values used with the ON DELETE clause in a referential constraint.

When ON DELETE CASCADE is specified, references in the child table to the parent record being deleted will cause the child records to also be deleted. If no action is specified, or if ON DELETE RESTRICT is specified, then the parent record cannot be deleted unless all child records which reference that record are first deleted. If the clause ON DELETE SET NULL is specified, the foreign key field will be set to NULL.

Here is a code example for reference:

```
CREATE TABLE "DBO"."HOSPITAL"   (
"HOSP_ID" INTEGER NOT NULL ,
"HOSP_NAME" CHAR(25) )
IN "USERSPACE1" ;

ALTER TABLE "DBO"."HOSPITAL"
ADD CONSTRAINT "PKeyHosp" PRIMARY KEY
("HOSP_ID");

CREATE TABLE "DBO"."PATIENT"   (
"PATIENT_ID" INTEGER NOT NULL ,
"PATIENT_NAME" CHAR(30) ,
"PATIENT_HOSP" INTEGER )
IN "USERSPACE1" ;

ALTER TABLE "DBO"."PATIENT"
ADD CONSTRAINT "PKeyPat" PRIMARY KEY
("PATIENT_ID");

ALTER TABLE "DBO"."PATIENT"
ADD CONSTRAINT "FKPatHosp" FOREIGN KEY
("PATIENT_HOSP")
REFERENCES "DBO"."HOSPITAL"
("HOSP_ID")
ON DELETE CASCADE;
```

38. Assume a table EMPLOYEE and you want to automatically archive any records that are deleted from this table to a new table EMPLOYEE_ARCHIVE. Assume the new table is defined correctly. Which DDL would you execute to begin archiving deleted records to table EMPLOYEE_ARCHIVE going forward?

To enable archiving of deleted records from table EMPLOYEE you would execute the following:

```
ALTER TABLE EMPLOYEE
ENABLE ARCHIVE
USE EMPLOYEE_ARCHIVE
```

39. Assume an EMPLOYEE table that includes a social security number field SSN. You want to mask the SSN value such that the true value is only shown to Human Relations staff who you will create an "HR" role for. All other users who access the field should see the mask XXX-XX-XXXX instead of the actual SSN.

To accomplish this, what function could you execute?

You would use the CREATE MASK function. Here is an example which includes the entire DDL:

```
CREATE ROLE HR;
ALTER TABLE EMPLOYEE ACTIVATE COLUMN ACCESS
CONTROL;

CREATE MASK SSN_MASK ON EMPLOYEE FOR
COLUMN SSN RETURN
CASE WHEN VERIFY_TRUSTED_CONTEXT_ROLE_FOR_USER
(SESSION_USER,'HR') = 1 THEN SSN
ELSE CHAR('XXX-XX-XXXX')
END
ENABLE
COMMIT;
```

40. Assume you have an application that needs to aggregate and summarize data from several tables multiple times per day. What special type of table could help improve performance of that application?

A materialized query table (MQT) is a table whose definition is based upon the result of a query, similar to a view. The difference is that the query on which a view is based is run each time the view is referenced. In contrast, an MQT actually stores the query results as data, and you can work with the data that is in the MQT instead of incurring the overhead of running a query which has to generate the data each time you run it. An MQT can

thereby significantly improve performance for applications that need summarized, aggregated data.

41. What is the schema for a GLOBAL TEMPORARY table?

The schema for a GLOBAL TEMPORARY table is always SESSION.

42. Name some reasons you might want to use a stored procedure?

- **Stored procedures can be used to reduce complexity by encapsulating business logic into modules.**

- **Using stored procedures can also improve performance and reduce network traffic.**

43. What is the default isolation level for DB2?

Cursor Stability is the default isolation level in DB2.

44. Which isolation level is most appropriate when few or no updates are expected to a table?

UR - Uncommitted Read uses less overhead than the other isolation levels and is most appropriate for read-only access of tables.

45. Name at least one clause that can be used to pull data for a particular period from a version enabled table?

Any of these clauses may be used to specify the time period on a query against a version enabled table:

FOR SYSTEM TIME AS OF

FOR SYSTEM TIME FROM...TO...

FOR SYSTEM TIME BETWEEN... AND...

46. Which data type is most appropriate for storing very large (over 1 MB) text strings?

    A CLOB (Character Large Object) is the best choice for storing very large (up to 2GB) character strings. Note that the CHAR type holds a maximum of 254 bytes. VARCHAR holds a maximum of 32,672 bytes.

47. Which authority has the most capabilities in DB2?

    The SYSADM authority has the most capabilities. SYSADM can issue any command against any DB2 instance, any database in the instance, and any object in the database. SYSADM can also access data within the databases.

48. Which clauses when used with ORDER BY will result in displaying data in reverse order from highest to lowest?

    DESC is short for descending, and when used with ORDER BY it means sort in descending order.

49. If you want to ensure that a value is assigned to a column even if the DML does not specify one, what clause would you use when you define the column?

The **DEFAULT** clause is used to specify a default value for a column. For example you could specify **DEFAULT** 0 for an integer column. This will ensure a value is assigned to a column even if the DML does not specify one.

50. Assume you have a long running process and you want to commit results after processing every 500 records, but have the ability to undoing any work after the commit point. One mechanism that would allow you to do this is to use what clause?

Issuing a SAVEPOINT enables you to execute several SQL statements as a single executable block. You can then undo changes back out to that savepoint by issuing a ROLLBACK TO SAVEPOINT statement.

51. Name a few advantages of using a trigger.

Advantages of using a trigger include:

- **Ability to write to other tables for audit trail.**

- **Ability to read other tables for validation.**

- **Ability to compare data before and after update operations.**

52. If you want a list of records that are in one table but not in a second table, name one or two clauses that would help you produce this list.

Two clauses that would produce the needed result are EXCEPT and NOT IN.

EXCEPT is used when you want a refined result set that includes all rows that are in result set 1 except for those that are in resultset-2. For example:

```
SELECT LASTNAME FROM TABLE1
EXCEPT (SELECT LNAME FROM TABLE2).
```

The **NOT IN** can be used in a similar way with a sub-select; for example:

```
SELECT LASTNAME
FROM TABLE1
WHERE LASTNAME NOT IN
(SELECT LNAME FROM TABLE2)
```

53. Name some clauses that when used in a field definition will prevent a column from having null values when the row is inserted.

- **NOT NULL** prevents a row from being added with a **NULL** value.

- **WITH DEFAULT** provides a **DEFAULT** value for the column which is used if no value is supplied when an **INSERT** is done.

- **GENERATED ALWAYS AS IDENTITY** means the column always has a numeric value generated by DB2, and therefore does not allow nulls.

54. In order to invoke a stored procedure, which keyword would you use?

CALL is the correct statement to invoke a stored procedure. The syntax is **CALL <procedure-name>**.

55. What operations or actions can end a unit of work?

A commit, a rollback, or the end of an application process can end a unit of work.

56. On a z/OS system, what is the usual encoding scheme used?

EBCDIC is typically used on z/OS systems.

57. If you find out that your application query is doing a table space scan, what changes could you make to improve the scan efficiency?

You could create one or more indexes on the search columns so that an index scan would occur instead of a tablespace scan.

58. Assume you want to update a table where some of the updates are for rows that already exist, but other rows do not yet exist and they need to be inserted. At run time you do not know which records exist and which do not exist. Which verb could you use to accomplish the INSERTS and UPDATES with a single SQL statement?

The merge statement is a combination of INSERT and UPDATE. For reference here is a coding example for updating the PAY column of the EMPLOYEE table as well as adding the EMPLOYEE record if it does not exist:

Here is a code example for reference:

```
MERGE INTO EMPLOYEE AS TARGET
USING (VALUES(:EMP_ID, :PAY_AMT))
AS SOURCE(EMPID, PAY)
```

```
ON TARGET.EMPID = SOURCE.EMPID
WHEN MATCHED THEN UPDATE SET TARGET.PAY =
SOURCE.PAY
WHEN NOT MATCHED THEN INSERT (EMPID, PAY)
VALUES (SOURCE.EMPID, SOURCE.PAY);
```

59. To end a transaction without making the changes permanent, which DB2 statement should be issued?

   Issuing a ROLLBACK statement will end a transaction without making the changes permanent.

60. Name some differences between static and dynamic SQL?

   - **The preparation of statements for dynamic SQL is determined at run time, not at bind time.**

   - **The access path for dynamic SQL is determined at run time.**

   - **Static SQL is generally a more secure environment than dynamic SQL.**

   - **Performance is generally better with static SQL than with dynamic SQL.**

61. What are some tools you can use to debug a stored procedure?

   - **When you change a stored procedure, remember that the WLM environment must be refreshed before the changes take effect.**

- The **DEBUG** Tool for z/OS can be used to debug stored procedures written in **C, C++, COBOL** or **PLI** languages.

- Issuing the **DISPLAY PROCEDURE** displays statistics about stored procedures accessed by **DB2** applications, including the status of each procedure.

62. Explain some ways of improving query performance?

- Evaluate stage two predicates to see if they can be rephrased as a stage 1 predicate.

- Create a needed index on the major search fields.

- Execute **RUNSTATS** and rebind application programs to make use of the latest information on the tables – this could improve the access path chosen in the **DB2** plan.

63. Identify and explain the use of the functions for operating on JSON data values?

- The **JSON_VAL** function is used to retrieve data that is inside a **JSON** document.

- The **JSON2BSON** function converts the specified **JSON** document in string format to an equivalent binary representation in **BSON** format.

- The **BSON2JSON** function converts a **BLOB** value in binary **BSON** format into a readable **JSON** text format.

64. Which keyword is used in a query to eliminate duplicate records from the result set?

    DISTINCT eliminates all except one of the duplicate rows in the result set. Rows are considered duplicates if the values for all columns selected by the query are equal.

65. Explain the difference between DML, DDL and DCL?

    Data Management Language is used to manipulate data in a table through use of the INSERT, UPDATE or DELETE keywords. Data Definition Language (DDL) is used to create, alter and drop database objects. Data Control Language (DCL) is used to grant and revoke access to database objects.

66. What isolation level is most likely to obtain a table level lock?

    REPEATABLE READ (RR) is more likely to obtain a table lock than the other isolation levels. Repeatable Read ensures that a query issued multiple times within the same unit of work will produce the exact same results. It does this by locking all rows that could affect the result, and does not permit any adds/changes/deletes to the table that could affect the result.

67. Which type of constraint would you use to ensure that a given column contains values between 1 and 365?

A CHECK constraint establishes some condition on a field, such as >= 10.

68. By default, how often does the IMPORT utility commit data?

The IMPORT utility commits data once at the end of the action. For large imports, it is recommended that you use the COMMITCOUNT option.

69. If you want to return the first 3 characters of a 10-character column, which function would you use?

SUBSTR returns a subset of the source string. The syntax is SUBSTR(X,Y, Z) where X is the source column, Y is the starting position, and Z is the length of the sub-string. Assuming a 10-character column FLD1, you would get the first three positions by coding SUBSTR(FLD1, 1,3).

70. To capture explain information for a dynamic SQL query without actually running the query, you should set the explain mode to what?

The explain mode for the query should be set to EXPLAIN when you want to capture explain information, but don't want to actually execute the query. The command is SET CURRENT EXPLAIN MODE EXPLAIN.

71. To determine who is using a DB2 instance, what command would you issue?

The LIST APPLICATIONS command returns the authority id and application (program) name of each attached application.

72. What are some situations in which you need to use a cursor in a program?

- **When your query will return more than one row.**

- **When you may need to update a row but need to examine the contents first.**

73. What is the primary item to check in the SQLCA area for the success or failure of the SQL statement?

The SQLCODE should be interrogated to determine the success or failure of an SQL statement. A zero indicates a successful query.

74. Name a situation when it is helpful to use a common table expression.

Some situations where a common table expression is useful are:

- **When the WHERE criteria is based on based on host variables.**

- **When the same result table needs to be shared in a fullselect.**

- **When the result needs to be derived using recursion.**

75. Which function would you use to return the smallest value in a set of values in a group.

The MIN function returns the smallest value in a set of values in a group.

76. To issue an embedded SQL statement in COBOL, what prefix must you use?

You enclose your SQL between EXEC SQL and END-EXEC keywords.

77. Which keyword does a common table expression start with?

A common table expression begins with the word "WITH", as in:

```
WITH
temp-table-name
AS(select a, b, c FROM table-D)
```

78. To remove all trailing blanks from a column, which function should be used in a query?

RTRIM removes all trailing blanks from a value, e.g., RTRIM(LASTNAME) would return the LASTNAME value minus any trailing spaces.

79. In a federated DB2 environment, what type of object is the local alias used to refer to databases at a particular data source?

In a federated DB2 environment, the NICKNAME is a local alias used to refer to a database at a particular data source.

80. If you want to combine two fields into a single field in a result set, what built-in routine would do this?

The CONCAT function combines two arguments. An example is as follows:

```
SELECT CONCAT(LASTNAME, " ,", FIRSTNAME)
FROM PEOPLE
WHERE LASTNAME = "SMITH"
and FIRSTNAME = 'JOHN'
```

81. In an embedded SQL program, if you use a SELECT INTO statement to place the values into host variables, and you are not using a cursor, what will happen?

If you are not using a cursor and your query returns more than one record, it will generate a -811 SQL code indicating this error condition. The error message is:

```
THE RESULT OF AN EMBEDDED SELECT STATEMENT OR A
SUBSELECT IN THE SET CLAUSE OF AN UPDATE STATEMENT IS A
TABLE OF MORE THAN ONE ROW, OR THE RESULT OF A SUBQUERY
OF A BASIC PREDICATE IS MORE THAN ONE VALUE.
```

82. When using a cursor, which statement do you use to cause the next row of the result set to be made available to the program?

FETCH causes the next row of the result set to be made available to the program.

83. When you retrieve an integer column you find that DB2 is suppressing leading zeros. You need the zeros to be displayed on a report. What function could you use to ensure that zeros are displayed for integer values?

The DIGITS function returns a character-string representation of the absolute value of a number. It consists exclusively of digits, including, if necessary, leading zeros to fill out the string.

84. Assume you have declared a cursor. Before you can issue a FETCH statement, you must issue which command?

After you declare a cursor, you must issue an OPEN statement before you can issue a FETCH.

85. Assume you have closed a cursor. What happens if you try to open it again?

A cursor can be closed and then opened again multiple times. Each time it is opened, it will behave as if it had not been used before.

86. Which table locks will prevent any other application from having any access to the table, including read access?

Super Exclusive(Z). The Z type lock prevents any other access to the table by other applications, including read access.

87. What is a composite key?

A composite key includes more than one column.

88. To grant a privilege to all users of the database, who would the grant be issued for?

Grant to PUBLIC. PUBLIC is a special "pseudo" group that means all users of the database.

89. To view the packages in a database using IBM Data Studio, which object would you need to select in the tree under the database name?

Packages are organized under the Application Objects node under the database name in the tree.

90. To include duplicate rows in a UNION clause, what additional keyword must you use?

UNION ALL will include duplicates. By default, UNION excludes duplicate entries, so the UNION keyword by itself will not include duplicates.

91. Which language would you use to grant access to database objects?

Data Control Language (DCL) is used to grant and revoke access to database objects.

92. In DB2 11 you can improve performance for read-only queries run against remote sites by binding with a new value for DBPROTOCOL. What is the new value that can be used when binding applications?

Binding applications with the new DBPROTOCOL (DRDACBF) option results in package-based continuous block fetch.

Package-based continuous block fetch provides a performance advantage for an application that produces large read-only result sets from a remote site.

93. DB2 11 introduced autonomous procedures. Name some characteristics of these procedures.

Characteristics of autonomous procedures include the following:

- Autonomous procedures run with their own units of work, separate from the calling program.

- If a calling program issues a ROLLBACK to back out its changes, the committed changes of the autonomous procedure are not affected.

- Only native SQL procedures can be defined as autonomous. Parallelism is disabled for autonomous procedures. An autonomous procedure cannot call another autonomous procedure.

94. Name some actions that could improve performance in a DB2 application?

- Parallel processing can significantly reduce response time by running parallel operations in a partitioned tablespace.

- The EXPLAIN function can be used to determine access paths that DB2 will use for an SQL statement, and thereby enable tuning for greater efficiency.

- Binding most applications with the **ISOLATION(CS)** and **CURRENTDATA(NO)** options will usually mean that **DB2** can release locks early and thereby improve concurrency of data access.

95. Explain the use of the HAVING and ROLLUP clauses with GROUP BY.

HAVING specifies a condition that must be true for a group to be included in the results.

ROLLUP adds additional "sub-total" rows to the result set.

96. Name some valid types of user-defined functions (UDF)?

The valid types of user defined functions are:

- An external scalar function is written in a programming language and returns a scalar value.

- An external table function is written in a programming language and returns a table to the subselect from which it was started.

- A sourced function is implemented by starting another function that exists at the server.

- An SQL scalar function is written exclusively in SQL statements and returns a scalar value.

- An SQL table function is written exclusively as an SQL RETURN statement and returns a set of rows.

COBOL Questions

1. How can you refer to a sub-string of the contents of a variable?

    Use the varname (x:y) notation where x represents the starting position and y represents the length of the string you want to extract. For example:

    ```
    Move SOC-SEC-NO (6:4) to SOC-SEC-LAST4.
    ```

2. Name some elements of the COBOL Identification division.

    The elements include Program-Id, Author, Installation, Date-Written, Date-Compiled.

    ```
    IDENTIFICATION DIVISION.
    Program-ID. PGM12345.
    Author. John Smith.
    Installation. Sunrise Programming.
    Date-Written. 06/12/2016.
    Date-Compiled. 06/14/2016.
    ```

3. What is a scope terminator?

    A scope terminator marks the end of a verb. For example: IF, END-IF. EVALUATE, END-EVALUATE;

4. Which clause do you use to define a table?

    Use the OCCURS clause to define a table. For example, to create a 50 element table and have it indexed by variable VAR1:

```
77 VAR1 USAGE IS INDEX.

01 SAMPLE-TABLE
   05  SAMPLE-COLUMN1 OCCURS 50 TIMES
       INDEXED BY VAR1.
       10  SAMPLE-FIELDA    PIC X (2).
       10  SAMPLE-FIELDB    PIC X (5).
```

5. What does the INITIALIZE keyword do?

    **INITIALIZE assigns default values for fields and is often
    used to initialize a structure variable with one statement
    instead of several. INITIALIZE moves zeros to
    alphanumeric fields and spaces to alphabetic fields.**

6. What is an inline PERFORM?

    **An inline PERFORM is a statement which is nested within
    a PERFORM statement itself (as opposed to being a
    separate paragraph). The inline perform is terminated by
    END-PERFORM.**

7. What is the LINKAGE SECTION used for?

    **The linkage section is used to pass data from one program
    to another program, or to receive data from a JCL.**

8. How can you determine whether a file is fixed block or variable
    blocked by looking at the COBOL program code?

    **Check the recording mode for the file in the program.
    RECORDING MODE F is fixed block. RECORDING
    MODE V is variable block.**

9. What is the difference between NEXT SENTENCE and CONTINUE?

    NEXT SENTENCE gives control to the verb following the next period.

    CONTINUE simply gives control to the next verb after the explicit scope terminator.

10. What needs to be done to force program to execute above the 16 Meg line?

    Make sure that link option is AMODE=31 and RMODE=ANY.

11. How do you send a return code from a COBOL program back to the executing JCL ?

    Move a value to the RETURN-CODE register. For example:

    ```
    MOVE 16 TO RETURN-CODE
    ```

12. What verb do you use to identify external files that the program will be using?

    Use the SELECT verb in the FILE-CONTROL part of the INPUT-OUTPUT SECTION of the ENVIRONMENT DIVISION. For example, if you want to relate the internal filename EMPLOYEE to it's JCL DDNAME which is EMPFILE. Here's is the syntax:

    ```
    SELECT EMPLOYEE ASSIGN TO AS-EMPFILE.
    ```

13. When using the MOVE verb, what happens if the target variable is shorter than the value being moved into it?

If the target variable is shorter than the value being moved into it, the value gets truncated on the right. So moving value "JOHNSON" into a PIC X(5) field would store "JOHNS".

14. If you want to trap a fixed overflow condition, what COBOL option will allow you to do this?

ON SIZE ERROR captures a fixed-point overflow. ON SIZE ERROR captures several other conditions as well:

- **Division by zero**
- **Zero raised to the zero power**
- **Zero raised to a negative number**
- **A negative number raised to a fractional power**
- **Floating-point overflow or underflow.**

15. How do you terminate an IF/ELSE statement?

Terminate an IF/ELSE statement with END-IF. For example:

```
IF NOT S-EOF
PERFORM 100-PROCESS-DATA
ELSE
PERFORM 400-PRINT-TOTALS
END-IF
```

16. If you want to load the current date to a variable TODAY-DATE defined as PIC X(8) and you want the date to be in YYYYMMDD format, what statement would accomplish this?

The following statement will load the current date to a variable TODAY-DATE and leave it in YYYYMMDD format:

```
Move Function Current-Date(1:8) to TODAY-DATE
```

17. What is an 88 level data element used for?

A level 88 is always associated with another variable. It is used to set up condition names based on the data. For example if you have a gender variable and you want to use the value in the field for later branching in the program, you could define it this way:

```
05  GENDER          PIC X.
    88  MALE    VALUE "M".
    88  FEMALE  VALUE "F".
```

Now you can short-cut checking the actual value of GENDER by simply coding:

```
IF MALE PERFORM XXX.
```

```
IF FEMALE PERFORM YYY.
```

18. How can you get the current date from system?

Use the function CURRENT-DATE.

19. If you have a three digit numeric edited picture and you want to suppress the printing of leading zeros, how would you define it?

You would use the character Z to suppress printing of leading zeros. For example:

```
01   NUM-VALUE   PIC 'ZZ9'.
```

20. What is the difference between a binary search and a sequential search?

In a binary search (SEARCH ALL) the table element key values must be in ascending or descending sequence. In a sequential search (SEARCH) the table is searched sequentially.

21. What are two or three ways you could set a numeric variable to zero?

You could INITIALIZE the variable.

You could MOVE ZERO TO the variable.

You could define it with the VALUE clause as having value 0.

22. What is the difference between COMP and COMP-3 data elements?

COMP-3 is stored in packed decimal format. COMP format is binary.

23. When declaring the Procedure Division, what keyword do you use to indicate your program will receive data from another program?

The USING keyword followed by a data structure name (as defined in the Linkage Section of the Data Division) indicates you will receive data from another program. Hereis an example assuming the EMPDATA is a data structure.

```
PROCEDURE DIVISION USING EMPDATA
```

24. Name the sections in the Data division?

- FILE SECTION
- WORKING-STORAGE SECTION
- LOCAL-STORAGE SECTION
- SCREEN SECTION
- REPORT SECTION
- LINKAGE SECTION

25. Suppose you have a character variable with both capital and lower case letters. You want to move the value to another field, but you also want to change the text to all capital letters on the target field. What COBOL statement will do this?

Use the Upper-case function. Here is an example of changing mixed case to upper case.

```
MOVE FUNCTION UPPER-CASE(FULL-NAME)
    TO FULL-NAME-CAPS.
```

26. Explain the meaning of a PIC 9v99 field.

PIC 9v99 is a three position number field which has two positions to the right of an implied decimal point.

27. If you are not certain how many entries a table should have, how would you create a variable length table?

You add a DEPENDING ON X option to the OCCURS clause, where X is a variable. For example you could make the table variable between 1 and 50 elements depending on the value of a record counter.

```
SAMPLE-TABLE
SAMPLE-COLUMN1 OCCURS 1 to 50 TIMES DEPENDING
ON REC-CNT.
10   SAMPLE-FIELDA      PIC X (2)
10   SAMPLE-FIELDB      PIC X (5)
```

28. How do you sort files in a COBOL program?

Use the SORT verb. Specify the sort work file, plus the input and output files. Specify the key used to sort.

Syntax:

```
SORT File-A ON ASCENDING/DESCENDING KEY key....
USING File-B
GIVING File-C.
```

File-A is the sort workfile. File-B is the input file for the SORT. File-3 is the outfile from the SORT.

29. How can you append records to a file that already has data in it?

   Open the file for EXTEND instead of for OUTPUT. The EXTEND mode means you'll add to the end of the file when you write.

30. If you want the compiler to flag subscripts that are out of range, which compile option should you use?

   Compile option SSRANGE must be specified if you want the compiler to do range checking. The default option is NOSSRANGE.

31. In COBOL, how do you call a program statically? How about dynamically?

   For STATIC calls just used the program name in quotes. Example:

   ```
   CALL 'PROG1' USING <arguments>
   ```

   For a DYNAMIC call you create a program name variable and use that in the CALL statement. For example:

   ```
   77 WS-PROGRAM PIC X(8) VALUE 'PROG2'.

   CALL WS-PROGRAM USING arguments
   ```

32. What type of picture can be used for alphanumeric data types?

Use PIC X for alphanumerics. For example, you can define a 10 byte alphanumeric variable called TEST-VAR as follows:

```
TEST-VAR   PIC X (10).
```

33. What is the difference between a sentence and a statement?

A sentence is a series of COBOL statements that ends with a period. A statement is a COBOL verb with operand, such as MOVE +9 TO PAGE-COUNT.

34. When you open a file in I-O mode, what verb is used to update a record?

The REWRITE verb is used with files opened in I-O mode.

35. If you want to replace certain characters in a data item with other characters, what verb would you use?

You would use the INSPECT verb. The following example replaces all commas with spaces:

```
INSPECT VAR1 REPLACING ALL "," BY SPACE.
```

36. What is needed to define a hexadecimal value in a PIC X variable declaration?

You must enclose the hex value in single quotes prefixed by X. For example:

```
77 TESTVAR PIC X VALUE X'E5'.
```

37. Name the 4 divisions in a COBOL program.

The four divisions in a COBOL program are:

- **IDENTIFICATION DIVISION**
- **ENVIRONMENT DIVISION**
- **DATA DIVISION**
- **PROCEDURE DIVISION**

38. What are the different modes for opening a file in COBOL?

Files can be opened for:

- **INPUT**
- **OUTPUT**
- **I-O**
- **EXTEND**

39. What is a 77 level data element used for?

A 77 level is a primary data item. It cannot be divided into subdivisions. Sometimes 77 level elements are used as counters or pseudo-constants.

40. If you wanted to concatenate several items from a structure and then move the result to a variable, what COBOL statement can do this?

The STRING statement concatenates several items from a structure into a single string. In the following example we create a full name by concatenating first, middle and last name, and then put the result in RPT-LINE.

```
STRING FIRST-NAME SPACE MIDDLE-NAME SPACE LAST-
NAME
DELIMITED BY SIZE
INTO RPT-LINE
WITH POINTER RPT-LINE-POS.
```

41. Name a few ways you can improve your program's performance.

These are a few ways to improve program performance. There are many others.

- Use the OPTIMIZE compile option.
- Use Computational variables wherever possible, and specify USAGE BINARY.
- Process tables with an index instead of a subscript.

42. What is the REDEFINES clause used for?

REDEFINES is used to allow the same storage allocation to be referenced by different data names. Here is an example where the first, middle and last names are basically concatenated together by redefining the space into a single variable:

```
TEST-NAME
05  FIRST   PIC X(15).
05  MIDDLE  PIC X(01).
05  LAST    PIC X(25).
ADDRESS PIC X(40).

FULL-NAME REDEFINES TEST-NAME
PIC X(41).
```

43. What is a COPYBOOK in COBOL?

A **COPYBOOK** is an external file which is included in the program source at compile time. It is used to store the code centrally and to share it across multiple programs. Copy books are often used for file layouts or common subroutines.

44. What does SET TO TRUE mean for an 88 level variable?

You can assign an 88 level value into its data element by setting the 88 level to **TRUE** (rather than explicitly moving a data value into the data element). For example if you **SET FEMALE TO TRUE** then **GENDER** will now contain "F.

```
05  GENDER          PIC X.
88  MALE        VALUE "M".
88  FEMALE      VALUE "F".
```

45. Explain what an EVALUATE statement is used for?

In **COBOL,** the **EVALUATE** verb implements the case construct. It can be used in place of nexted IFs to make code less complex and more readable. An example of **EVALUATE** is:

```
EVALUATE GENDER
WHEN "M"
MOVE "MALE" TO PRINT-GENDER
WHEN "F"
MOVE "FEMALE" TO PRINT-GENDER
WHEN OTHER
MOVE "UNKNOWN" TO PRINT-GENDER
END-EVALUATE
```

46. What is the difference between performing a SECTION and performing a PARAGRAPH?

Performing a SECTION will cause all the paragraphs that are in the section to be performed.

Performing a PARAGRAPH will cause only that paragraph to be performed.

47. If you have a complex arithmetic calculation, which verb could you use to perform the calculation with a single statement?

You can use the COMPUTE statement for most arithmetic evaluations, and often you can use a single COMPUTE statement rather than multiple ADD, SUBTRACT, MULTIPLY, and DIVIDE statements. For example:

```
Compute TOTAL = a + b / c ** d - e
```

48. What is level 66 used for ?

It is used with the RENAMES clause. You use it to reference another variable. A 66 level is placed at the end of the record structure.. Example where we rename a few fields into the 66 level for convenience. Now we can reference the first three fields by one name, FULL-NAME.

```
01  TEST-NAME
        05  FIRST   PIC X(15).
        05  MIDDLE  PIC X(01).
        05  LAST    PIC X(25).
        05  ADDRESS PIC X(40).

66 FULL-NAME RENAMES FIRST THRU LAST.
```

49. Which compile option would you use to get a listing of all the items in the Data Division?

Use the MAP compile option to create a listing of all the items in the DATA Division.

50. If you want the compile listing to include diagnostics only for severity levels Warning and higher, what compile option would you use?

You would use FLAG(W) to include diagnostics only for severity levels Warning and higher. The values for the FLAG compile option are as follows:

```
I - Informational
W - Warning
E - Error
S - Severe Error
U - Unrecoverable
```

PLI Questions

1. If you are performing arithmetic calculations, which data type usually performs best?

    Use of FIXED BINARY generally has a faster performance than using other numeric types.

2. What is an example of an ON condition and what it is used for?

    An ON condition is a situation in a PLI program that could cause a program interrupt. Examples include unexpected errors such as a fixed variable overflow, or encountering the end of a file when reading. PLI programs can be coded to trap these conditions. In the case of the end of file condition, here is an example of code to turn off a more-records switch when end of file is encountered (to avoid the error of reading past the end of file).

    ```
    ON ENDFILE(TRANS)
       S_MORE_RECORDS = NO;
    ```

3. What is the difference between a PLI function and a PLI procedure?

    A function returns a value to the calling procedure. A procedure does not return a value.

4. Name some ON conditions that are raised by invalid arithmetic operations?

   A few of these are CONVERSION, FIXEDOVERFLOW and ZERODIVIDE.

5. What verb is used to implement the case control structure in a PL/1 program?

   The SELECT statement implements the CASE structure. The syntax is:

   ```
   SELECT (optional expression);
      WHEN (expression) action 1;
      WHEN (expression) action 2;
      OTHERWISE action 3
   END;
   ```

6. What is the difference between a DO WHILE control structure and a DO UNTIL control structure?

   DO WHILE checks its loop control condition at the top of the loop, while DO UNTIL checks at the bottom. The DO UNTIL is always executed at least once.

   Also, the DO UNTIL is terminated when it's loop condition is TRUE whereas a DO WHILE is terminated when it's loop condition is FALSE.

7. If you define the logical record length of a file to be 133 in your program, and actual record length is 132, what condition will be raised?

   The RECORD condition is raised when there is a discrepancy between the declared and actual file

specification. This includes a discrepancy between the declared and actual LRECL on a file.

8. What value can you use in a picture clause to suppress leading zeros when a numeric field is printed?

   The Z character is used to suppress leading zeros, such as in:

   ```
   DCL VAR1 PIC 'ZZZ9' INIT
   ```

9. If you have a structure and you want to declare a second structure identically without specifying the details, what keyword could you use to do this?

   Use the LIKE keyword to define a structure exactly the same as another structure. For example, the substructure under EMPL_B will be implicitly the same as EMPL_A below:

   ```
   DCL  01 EMPL_A,
   05   LNAME     CHAR (30),
   05   FNAME     CHAR (20),
   05   MI        CHAR (01);

   DCL  01 EMPL_B   LIKE EMPL_A;
   ```

10. How would one use the built-in function INDEX?

    INDEX searches a string for a specified bit or character configuration. If it is found, the starting location will be returned. If not found, zero will be returned.

11. What is a good way to terminate a DO LOOP without using a GOTO statement?

Assuming you are using a numeric loop control variable, you can set the variable to make the loop control condition false. For example you can terminate this loop when the loop counter exceeds 9 as follows:

```
DO A = 1 to 100;
    IF A > 9 THEN
        A = 100;
    ELSE
        PUT SKIP LIST (A);
END;
```

12. How would one use the VERIFY function?

VERIFY examines two strings to verify that each character or bit in the first string is represented in the second string. It returns a 0 if true, otherwise it returns the position of the first character in the first string that is not in the second string.

For example one could declare a character string named NUMERICS with the digits 0 thru 9:

```
DCL 01 NUMERICS CHAR(10) INIT('0123456789');
```

Now given a variable named EMPLOYEE_ID, we can check for numeric using this code:

```
IF VERIFY(EMPLOYEE_ID,NUMERICS) = 0 THEN
```

If the result is not zero, then the result will be the position of the first character in EMPLOYEE_ID that is not in NUMERICS.

13. What are the most commonly used data types in PLI?

- **FIXED BIN**
- **FIXED DEC**
- **FLOAT BIN**
- **FLOAT DEC**
- **CHAR**
- **BIT**
- **NUMERIC (PIC)**

14. If you want to display something in the output of your program run, what verbs will you use?

You would use the PUT LIST (*variable or constant to display*). For example, if you wanted to display the value of variable EMP_NAME with a literal in front of it, you could code:

```
PUT SKIP LIST
('EMPLOYEE NAME = ' || EMP_NAME);
```

15. Explain the SUBSTR function – how does it work and what is it used for?

SUBSTR is a string handling function used to extract part of a string. SUBSTR has three arguments: (1) the string from which to extract the data, (2) the starting position in the string, (3) the number of characters to extract. For example suppose you have a CHAR variable X that you want to extract the first three bytes from and store it in CHAR variable Y. You could code this:

```
Y = SUBSTR(X,1,3);
```

16. What is the use of the DEFINED attribute in the declare statement of a variable?

The DEFINED attribute indicates that the variable is mapped on storage of another variable. For example you could declare an 80 byte DATA_AREA variable, and then a separate KEY_FIELD variable of length 10 that begins in position 12 of the DATA_AREA. Here is a code example:

```
DCL    DATA_AREA  CHAR(80) INIT(' ');
DCL    KEY_FIELD  CHAR(10) DEF DATA_AREA POS(12);
```

17. What is the difference between DEFINED attribute and LIKE attribute?

The DEFINED attribute maps the variable to storage of another variable. The LIKE attribute allocates new storage similar to another variable.

18. What PLI function enables you to initiate a program trace that will display a listing of procedures called and variable values when they change?

Use the PLI keyword CHECK enclosed in parentheses and followed by a colon, right before the procedure you are tracing. For example:

```
(CHECK):
CALC:   PROCEDURE OPTIONS(MAIN);
<add logic here>
END CALC;
```

19. If your program abends on a TRANSMIT condition, what is the likely cause?

A TRANSMIT condition means that an I/O device (such as a tape drive) did not move the data correctly. The usual cause of this is a hardware problem.

20. What is the difference between built-in function VERIFY and INDEX?

INDEX(x,y) returns the starting position of the string y within string x. It returns 0 if y is not present in x.

Verify(x,y) returns the first position in x where any character in y is not in string 1. If all characters in x are contained in y, the result is zero.

21. How do you include a copybook?

Use the %INCLUDE verb followed by the member name of the copybook:

```
%INCLUDE FILE1234;
```

22. What is the PLI symbol for exponentiation?

The symbol is a double asterisk **. For example:

X ** 3

means X raised to the third power.

23. How do you concatenate two string variables in PLI?

The concatenation symbol is two vertical marks | | and is placed between the items to be concatenated. For example you could concatenate first and last names with a space between them:

```
FNAME = 'JOHN' ;
LNAME = 'SMITH' ;
FULL_NAME = FNAME || ' ' || LNAME ;
```

24. What result does the ABS builtin function return?

ABS returns the absolute value of a number.

25. When an interrupt condition occurs, what function can be called to determine the type of interrupt?

ONCODE can be called to indicate the type of interrupt. Typically you would display this using PUT. For example:

```
ON ERROR
PUT LIST (ONCODE) ;
```

26. When an interrupt condition occurs, what function can be called to indicate the procedure name where the interrupt occurred?

ONLOC can be called to indicate the procedure name where the interrupt occurred. You can print out both the ONCODE and ONLOC as follows:

```
ON ERROR
PUT LIST (ONCODE, ONLOC) ;
```

27. If you want to declare an array of 100 elements of CHAR(04) and call the array TABLE1, how would you code it?

You would code it as follows:

```
DCL    TABLE1 (100)    CHAR(04);
```

28. If you want to test your program's general error-handling logic, but you don't want to actually create all the conditions that might occur, what PLI verb can you use to simulate the conditions you want to test?

Use the SIGNAL verb with whatever ON conditions you want to test. If you want to simulate an error condition, you would code:

```
SIGNAL ERROR;
```

29. What does the MOD function do?

MOD gives the remainder resulting from dividing the first argument by the second argument. For example:

MOD(35,17) results in a value of 1 because 35 divided by 17 is 2 with a remainder of 1.

MOD(25,5) results in a value of zero because 25 divided by 5 equals zero with no remainder.

30. If you wanted to develop a two dimensional array of 100 elements (dimension one) by 12 elements (dimension two) of

CHAR(04) and call the array TABLE2, how would you code it?

You would code it as follows:

```
DCL    TABLE1 (100, 12)    CHAR(04);
```

31. What is the CONTROLLED keyword used for?

    The CONTROLLED keyword is a variable attribute used to create a STACK. Scalar variables, arrays and structures can be declared with the CONTROLLED attribute. An example of a variable declared with the CONTROLLED attribute is:

```
DCL ERROR_MESSAGE CHAR(50) CONTROLLED;
```

32. How is storage for a CONTROLLED variable created and released? Give an example.

    Storage for a CONTROLLED variable is created by used of the ALLOCATE verb, and released by use of the FREE verb. Here is an example of creating a stack named ERROR_MESSAGE, adding two messages to it, and then printing and clearing the messages from the stack.

```
DCL   ERROR_MESSAGE   CHAR(50) CONTROLLED;

ALLOCATE ERROR_MESSAGE;
ERROR_MESSAGE = "INVALID NAME";
ALLOCATE ERROR_MESSAGE;
ERROR_MESSAGE = "INVALID DATE";
```

```
PUT SKIP LIST (ERROR_MESSAGE);
FREE ERROR_MESSAGE;
PUT SKIP LIST (ERROR_MESSAGE);
FREE ERROR_MESSAGE;
```

The output will be:

```
INVALID DATE
INVALID NAME
```

33. What syntax would you used to declare a dynamic array?

Use an asterisk instead of a finite number of elements when allocating the array. For example:

```
DCL TEST_ARRAY(*) CHAR(4);
```

34. What is the standard system action taken when an ERROR condition is raised?

The standard system action taken when an **ERROR** condition is raised is to terminate the **PLI** program and return control to the operating system. You can override this action by intercepting the **ERROR** condition with an **ON ERROR** statement. For example:

```
ON ERROR
    PUT SKIP LIST
    ('The program encountered an error');
```

35. What does the FETCHABLE attribute mean?

When you want a sub-program to have the ability to be called dynamically at run time, declare that program with **OPTIONS(FETCHABLE)** instead of **OPTIONS(MAIN)**. The sub-program must then be loaded into memory by the calling program using the FETCH verb. Once loaded, the sub-program can be called normally like any other sub-program.

36. When a variable's value has to be maintained across several executions of a procedure, how should the variable be declared?

    The variable should be declared with the STATIC attribute. Doing so ensures that the value will not be reinitialized each time the procedure is called. Example:

    ```
    DCL   VALUE1    FIXED BIN (31)   STATIC;
    ```

37. What does LIFO stand for and what storage structure is it implemented with?

    LIFO refers to a last in – first out order of processing. This is typically implemented as a STACK where the last value placed on the stack is the first value to be retrieved from it.

38. What is the basic syntax to declare a file named TESTFILE for record type input?

    ```
    DCL TESTFILE FILE RECORD INPUT;
    ```

39. What is the basic syntax to declare a file named OUTFILE for stream type output?

```
DCL OUTFILE FILE STREAM OUTPUT;
```

40. What carriage control character would you use to skip to the top of the next page?

The number "1" carriage control character means to skip to the next page.

41. Suppose you have a VSAM file declared as follows:

```
DCL PAYFILE FILE INPUT
    RECORD KEYED ENV(VSAM);
```

What is the syntax to read the record having the key value stored in EMPLOY_NUM from this file into structure EMPLOY_REC?

The syntax for read the record having the key value stored in EMPLOY_NUM from PAYFILE into structure EMPLOY_REC is as follows:

```
READ FILE(PAYFILE) INTO (EMPLOY_REC)
KEY(EMPLOY_NUM);
```

42. What condition will be raised if you try to open a file that is not defined in your execution JCL?

The UNDEFINEDFILE condition will be raised when the opening of a file fails due to not being defined in the JCL.

43. What condition will be raised if you try to read a record using a key value for which there is no record?

The **KEY** condition will be raised if a keyed record cannot be found on a read operation.

44. What is the difference between an argument and a parameter?
An argument is a value passed to a called procedure. A parameter is a declaration of a value to be received in the called procedure. The attributes of a passed argument and received parameter must be the same.

45. What keyword terminates a PLI function?

The RETURN keyword not only terminates a function but also passes back a value to the calling procedure.

46. What value does the pointer variable of the last element of a linked list contain?

PLI refers to the end of a linked list as NULL. This is because pointer variable from the last item in the list has the special value NULL which specifically means the end of the list. NULL must be declared with the BUILTIN attribute to be valid.

47. What are the two ways a procedure can end normally?

The procedure ends normally either by reaching the END statement for the procedure or by a RETURN statement. Either way control is passed back to the calling procedure.

48. If your program needs to suspend execution for a specified period of time, which verb will accomplish this?

The **DELAY** verb will suspend program execution for the number of milliseconds specified. For example to pause the program for 10 seconds, issue this statement:

```
DELAY(delay (10000);
```

49. What statement specifies the action to be taken in a SELECT statement if none of the WHEN conditions is satisfied?

The OTHERWISE clause (if coded) specifies the action to be taken in a SELECT statement if none of the WHEN conditions is satisfied.

```
SELECT (optional expression);
WHEN (expression) action 1;
WHEN (expression) action 2;
OTHERWISE action 3
END;
```

50. If you are reading a file and you want to skip a certain number of records, what clause would you use with the READ statement?

You would use the IGNORE clause. For example if you are reading file INFILE and want to skip two records and then read the third record you would code it as follows:

```
READ FILE (INFILE) IGNORE (2);
```

CICS Questions

1. What does the CICS acronym stand for?

   CICS basically stands for Customer Information Control System.

2. In which programming languages can you develop CICS programs?

   COBOL, Assembler, PLI, Java and C/C++

3. What three services does CICS provide to handle data?

   File control, DL/I (for IMS data) and SQL (for DB2 data).

4. What is BMS?

   BMS is Basic Map Support. It allows you to code assembler level programs to define screens.

5. What is the difference between the PCT and the PPT in CICS?

   PCT means Program Control Table. It includes all transactions and the corresponding programs that are defined to CICS.

   PPT means Processing Program Table. It includes those programs that are loaded in storage.

6. What is the TCT?

   **The terminal control table defines all terminals that use
   CICS in the installation.**

7. What is the FCT?

   **FCT stands for File Control Table and it provides an
   accounting of all files defined to CICS along with the file
   type, record length and status of the file.**

8. In a COBOL program, how are CICS commands enclosed?

   **CICS commands are coded between the EXEC CICS and
   END-EXEC statements. For example:**

   ```
   EXEC CICS
           ABEND
   END-EXEC.
   ```

9. What are the CICS commands for handling screen interactions?

   RECEIVE MAP – Retrieves input from the terminal.

   SEND MAP – Sends information to the terminal.

10. What does the symbolic map include?

    **It includes (in COBOL) two 01 level structures, one for
    input and one for output.**

11. What is the difference between a physical BMS mapset and a BMS symbolic mapset?

The physical mapset is a load module used to map the data to the screen at execution time. The symbolic map is the actual copybook member used in the program to reference the input and output fields on the screen.

12. What are the two assembler commands that are required to code a BMS mapset?

The two required assembler commands are:

```
PRINT NOGEN

END
```

13. What are the three macros used in building a mapset?

The three macros used in building a mapset are:

- **DFHMSD starts the mapset.**

- **DFHMDI starts a map within the mapset.**

- **DFHMDF defines each field within a map.**

14. What attributes are used to make a field normal intensity on the screen and protected (so that the field cannot change)?

The attribute value for this scenario is coded as:

```
ATTRB=(NORM,PROT)
```

15. What are the CICS commands that transfer control from one program to another?

LINK – calls a program at a lower level of the calling chain.

XCTL – calls a program without a return link.

RETURN – returns control to a calling program or to CICS.

ABEND – transfers control to an abend process or to CICS.

16. What attribute will cause the cursor to be placed on a field when the screen displays?

Use the IC attribute value to cause the cursor to be placed on a field when the screen displays. For example:

```
ATTRB=(NORM,UNPROT,IC)
```

17. Which EIB field contains the length of the data that was passed to the program?

The EIBCALEN field contains the length of the data that was passed to the program.

18. What CICS command is used to access current date and time?

The ASKTIME command moves the date and time values to fields EIBDATE and EIBTIME respectively.

19. The CICS commands for processing VSAM files are:

- **WRITE** – Adds a record.

- **READ** – retrieves a record.

- **DELETE** – deletes a record.

- **REWRITE** – updates a record.

- **SYNCPOINT** – commits data updates.

- **SYNCPOINT(ROLLBACK)** rolls back all data updates.

20. Explain how the EIBAID field is used

EIBAID is a key field in the execute interface block. You can check EIBAID field to know which AID key the user has pressed (for example the ENTER key or the PA3 key).

21. What is the EXEC CICS HANDLE CONDITION command used for?

The HANDLE CONDITION command specifies the paragraph or program label to which control is to be passed if the condition occurs. For example:

```
EXEC CICS HANDLE CONDITION
    NOTFND(C9000-RECORD-NOT-FOUND)
    ERROR(C9900-ERROR)
END-EXEC.
```

22. What typically causes a MAPFAIL condition when processing a RECEIVE MAP command?

When no data was sent from the screen, this raises a MAPFAIL condition.

23. The communication or COMMAREA must be included in the Linkage section of the program. What is the required name for this field in the Linkage section?

The area must be defined as the first area in the Linkage Section and must be called DFHCOMMAREA.

24. What is the syntax of the RECEIVE MAP command?

The syntax of the RECEIVE MAP command is as follows:

```
EXEC CICS
  RECEIVE MAP (map name)
              MAPSET(map set name)
              INTO (data name)

END-EXEC.
```

So for example if your mapset name is EMPMS01 and your map is named EMPM02, and your data structure name is EMPMAP1, you would code:

```
EXEC CICS
  RECEIVE MAP (EMPM02)
          MAPSET(EMPMS01)
          INTO (EMPMAP1)
END-EXEC.
```

25. When do you need to use the NEWCOPY keyword?

You use NEWCOPY with CEMT to bring the latest version of the program from the loadlib into CICS.

For example, to bring latest version of program EMPPGM1 into storage, issue:

```
CEMT SET PROGRAM(EMPPGM1)NEWCOPY
```

26. What is the difference between FSET and FRSET?

FSET specifies that the modified data tag bit for each unprotected field should be turned on before the map is sent to the screen.

FRSET specifies to turn off the modified data bit of the unprotected fields. This is to ensure that only data that has been modified since the last send will be transmitted.

27. What is the difference between an EXEC CICS HANDLE CONDITION command and an EXEC CICS IGNORE command?

The HANDLE CONDITION command traps the condition and transfers control to a paragraph that will perform some action.

The IGNORE command simply passes control to the next sequential instruction following the command which raised the condition, i.e., it ignores the condition.

28. What is the syntax of the XCTL command?

The syntax of the XCTL command is:

```
EXEC CICS
        XCTL PROGRAM (program name)
END-EXEC.
```

29. What is the syntax of the RETURN command?

The syntax of the RETURN command is:

```
EXEC CICS
        RETURN [TRANSID(transaction id)]
          COMMAREA(working storage comm area)
END-EXEC.
```

30. If a CICS program calls another program using the LINK
    command, what syntax of the RETURN command can the called
    program use to return control to the calling program?

**If a CICS program calls another program using the LINK
command, the called program need only use the RETURN
command without any options.**

```
EXEC CICS
        RETURN
END-EXEC.
```

31. On a SEND command, what happens if you don't specify
    MAPONLY or DATAONLY?

**Both constant data from the physical map and modifiable
data from the symbolic map are sent.**

32. What is the syntax to disable a transaction using the CEMT command?

The syntax to disable a transaction using the CEMT command is:

```
CEMT S TRANS(transid) DIS
```

33. Assume one program calls another using a COMMAREA and you want the called program to be able to modify the COMMAREA and have the changes reflected in the calling program. Would you use XCTL or LINK to accomplish this?

You would need to use the LINK command because the DFHCOMMAREA in the called program refers to the same storage as that used by the calling program. So changes made to the DFHCOMMAREA by the called program are reflected in the calling program's COMMAREA when control is returned to that calling program.

If you use XCTL to call a program, only a copy of the COMMAREA is passed to the called program, so any changes made in the latter will not be reflected in the calling program. In fact when XCTL is used, the calling program's memory is released since control will not be returned to it.

34. What is the syntax to issue an abend command that specifies AZ99 as the abend code?

The syntax to issue an abend command that specifies AZ99 as the abend code:

```
EXEC CICS
  ABEND ABCODE(AZ99)
END-EXEC.
```

35. What is the syntax of the READ command when you intend to update the record later?

The syntax of the READ command when you intend to update the record is as follows:

```
EXEC CICS
        READ FILE (file name)
        INTO (data structure name)
        RIDFLD(field name)
        UPDATE
        RESP(RESPONSE-CODE)
END-EXEC.
```

36. What type of condition will be raised if you try to read a file that you do not have authorization for?

The NOTAUTH condition will be raised if you try to read a file that you do not have authorization for.

37. How can you intercept and code for errors in CICS programs?

One way to handle error conditions is to check for them by interrogating the EIBRESP after an action. Another way is to code HANDLE to intercept conditions and branch to a routine to handle the conditions.

38. What CICS command returns the user's logonid?

The command to get the user logonid and store it in a field named WS-USERID is:

```
EXEC CICS ASSIGN USERID(WS_USERID)
```

39. When an application program issues an EXEC CICS RECEIVE MAP command and there is no data sent back to the application program, what except will be raised?

When an application program issues an EXEC CICS RECEIVE MAP command and there is no data sent back, a MAPFAIL condition will be raised.

40. Which takes precedence, a HANDLE CONDITION command or a HANDLE AID command?

HANDLE AID takes precedence over HANDLE CONDITION.

41. If an application READS a VSAM KSDS file with UPDATE, and decides not to update the record, what command can be issued to release exclusive control on the record?

Issuing an EXEC CICS UNLOCK FILE (*filename*) command with the File or Dataset option will release control of the record. The lock will also be released if another READ is issued to move to another record.

42. What error will you receive if you issue an XCTL or a LINK command and the called program cannot be found?

A PGMIDERR condition will be raised if you issue an XCTL or a LINK command and the called program cannot be found.

43. What exceptional condition will be raised if you try to insert a record into a file and a record with the same key is already there?

   A DUPREC condition will be raised if you try to insert a record into a file and a record with the same key is already there.

44. If you want to use the STARTBR command to initiate a browse of the EMPLOYEE file at key in field START-KEY and store the response code in field RESP-CODE, what would the syntax of this command be?

   The syntax would be:

```
EXEC CICS
        STARTBR FILE ('EMPLOYEE')
        RIDFLD(START-KEY)
        RESP(RESP-CODE)
END-EXEC.
```

In this case the browse will begin at the first record equal to or greater than the specified key.

45. On a STARTBR command, what clause do you include with the RIDFLD to specify the browse *must* begin at a specific record?

   You include the EQUAL clause. If the record is not found then the browse will fail with NOTFND. An example is:

```
EXEC CICS
        STARTBR FILE ('EMPLOYEE')
        RIDFLD(START-KEY)
        EQUAL
        RESP(RESP-CODE)
END-EXEC.
```

46. What command do you issue to end a VSAM file browse?

You use the ENDBR command to end a browse and release the VSAM resources that are allocated to it. The syntax is:

```
EXEC CICS
     ENDBR FILE ('EMPLOYEE')
END-EXEC.
```

47. If you want to use only part of a key to browse a file, how could you do this?

You would use the KEYLENGTH clause with the STARTBR command. For example, if an EMPLOYEE file has an 8 position employee number EMP-NUM and you want to return all records where the first 4 characters match the first four characters in EMP-KEY, code the following:

```
EXEC CICS
    STARTBR FILE ('EMPLOYEE')
    RIDFLD(EMP-KEY)
    GENERIC
    KEYLENGTH(4)
    RESP(RESP-CODE)
END-EXEC.
```

48. What communication protocol enables a web application to connect to CICS on a mainframe computer?

Communication between web servers and mainframe computers running CICS is accomplished using TCP/IP.

49. What does the HANDLE AID command do?

HANDLE AID tells the program what step to take when the user presses one of the attention keys. For example this is how you would code a command to transfer control to a routine 1000-PF3-ACTION when the PF3 key is pressed.

```
EXEC CICS
        HANDLE AID PF3 (1000-PF3-ACTION)
        CLEAR
END-EXEC.
```

50. If you have read a record from the file EMPLOYEE with the UPDATE option, and you want to delete that record, what is the syntax?

The syntax to delete a record that has been read for update, and to assign the response code to field RESP-CODE is:

```
EXEC CICS
        DELETE FILE ('EMPLOYEE')
        RESP(RESP-CODE)
END-EXEC.
```

If you have not already read the record for update, you can delete it by specifying the RIDFLD option for the key.

Thanks for your purchase of this book. If you feel that this Interview Questions resource helped you in preparing for your IBM interview, please leave a positive book review at the place you bought it.

I'll really appreciate that! Thanks!

Other Titles by Robert Wingate

DB2 Exam C2090-320 Practice Questions

ISBN 13: 978-1539715405
This book will help you pass IBM Exam C2090-320 and become an IBM
Certified Database Associate - DB2 11 Fundamentals for z/OS. The 189
questions and answers in the book (three full practice exams) offer you a
significant advantage by helping you to gauge your readiness for the exam, to
better understand the objectives being tested, and to get a broad exposure to the
DB2 11 knowledge you'll be tested on.

DB2 Exam C2090-313 Practice Questions

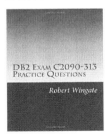

ISBN 13: 978-1534992467
This book will help you pass IBM Exam C2090-313 and become an IBM
Certified Application Developer - DB2 11 for z/OS. The 180 questions and
answers in the book (three full practice exams) offer you a significant advantage
by helping you to gauge your readiness for the exam, to better understand the
objectives being tested, and to get a broad exposure to the DB2 11 knowledge
you'll be tested on.

DB2 Exam C2090-615 Practice Questions

ISBN 13: 978-1535028349

This book will help you pass IBM Exam C2090-615 and become an IBM Certified Database Associate (DB2 10.5 for Linux, Unix and Windows). The questions and answers in the book offer you a significant advantage by helping you to gauge your readiness for the exam, to better understand the objectives being tested, and to get a broad exposure to the knowledge you'll be tested on.

DB2 10.1 Exam 610 Practice Questions

ISBN 13: 978-1-300-07991-0

This book will help you pass IBM Exam 610 and become an IBM Certified Database Associate. The questions and answers in the book offer you a significant advantage by helping you to gauge your readiness for the exam, to better understand the objectives being tested, and to get a broad exposure to the knowledge you'll be tested on.

DB2 10.1 Exam 611 Practice Questions

ISBN 13: 978-1-300-08321-4

This book will help you pass IBM Exam 611 and become an IBM Certified Database Administrator. The questions and answers in the book offer you a significant advantage by helping you to gauge your readiness for the exam, better understand the objectives being tested, and get a broad exposure to the knowledge you'll be tested on.

DB2 9 Exam 730 Practice Questions: Second Edition

ISBN-13: 978-1463798833

This book will help you pass IBM Exam 730 and become an IBM Certified Database Associate. The questions and answers in the book offer you a significant advantage by helping you to gauge your readiness for the exam, to better understand the objectives being tested, and to get a broad exposure to the knowledge you'll be tested on.

DB2 9 Certification Questions for Exams 730 and 731: Second Edition

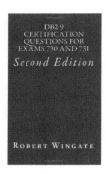

ISBN-13: 978-1466219755

This book is targeted for IBM Certified Database Administrator candidates for DB2 9 for Windows, Linux and UNIX. It includes approximately 400 practice questions and answers for IBM Exams 730 and 731 (6 complete practice exams).

About the Author

Robert Wingate is a computer services professional with over 30 years of IBM mainframe and distributed programming experience. He holds several IBM certifications, including IBM Certified Application Developer - DB2 11 for z/OS, and IBM Certified Database Administrator for LUW. Robert lives in Fort Worth, Texas.

Made in the USA
Las Vegas, NV
01 September 2024

94620251R10077